Empowering Employees Through

Basic Skills Training

MARCIA WEAVER

QUALITY RESOURCES®
A Division of The Kraus Organization Limited
New York, New York

Most Quality Resources books are available at quantity discounts when purchased in bulk. For more information contact:

Special Sales Department
Quality Resources
A Division of The Kraus Organization Limited
902 Broadway
New York, New York 10010
800-247-8519

Printed in the United States of America

00 99 98 97 96   10 9 8 7 6 5 4 3 2 1

Quality Resources
A Division of The Kraus Organization Limited
902 Broadway
New York, New York 10010
212-979-8600
800-247-8519

∞
The paper used in this publication meets the minimum requirements of American National Standard for Information Sciences—Permanence of Paper for Printed Library Materials, ANSI Z39.48-1984.

ISBN 0-527-76297-0

Library of Congress Cataloging-in-Publication Data

Weaver, Marcia Ruth, 1954–
    Basic skills training : a guide to preparing employees for quality improvement / Marcia Weaver.
        p.   cm.
    Includes index.
    ISBN 0-527-76297-0 (alk. paper)
    1. Total quality management—Study and teaching—Handbooks, manuals, etc. 2. Pioneer Electronics Technology, Inc.—Employees—Training of—Case studies. 3. Toro Company—Employees—Training of—Case studies. I. Title.
    HD62.15.W423   1996
    658.5'62'0715—dc20   95-51759
                                                              CIP

DEDICATION

This work is dedicated to the employees of The Toro Company, Irrigation Division and Pioneer Electronics Technology, Inc. who have the courage and the desire to learn and grow; all of the workers in the United States of America who are taking the risk of saying, "I don't know. Teach me. I want to increase my competence and my self-esteem."; and companies who are investing in training for their employees, who are taking pride in their achievements.

CONTENTS

PREFACE

My involvement with basic workplace skills came about unexpectedly and reinforced my long-time belief that everything you do in life comes back to serve you in some way. Before I began consulting in business, I taught in the California public school system for 11 years and then owned and managed two small retail stores. The last year and a half of my teaching experience involved working on teams to create subject matter competencies for the school district where I was employed. When I left teaching, I thought that teaching reading, writing, and math was something I had done in the past, but would probably never do again.

I had been consulting to businesses for eight years when I was offered the opportunity to submit a proposal for the basic workplace skills assessment and program implementation at The Toro Company, Irrigation Division in Riverside, California. The division had begun a Crosby-based quality improvement initiative. Planning for this initiative revealed significant deficits in basic skills that needed to be addressed if the initiative was to be successful. For Toro, the success of this quality initiative was crucial to remaining competitive in the long term. I was truly fortunate to be working with the team at Toro who were able to see in advance the challenges ahead for their workforce. They were willing to tackle the skills issues head-on, with maximum concern for the impact on their employees. It was an ideal environment in which to develop such a program.

As a result of the Toro program, I was referred to Pioneer Electronics Technology, Inc. (PET), a company in search of a vehicle for improving the educational level of its loyal, long-term, and in many cases, non-English-speaking workforce as the organization embarked on a certification effort for ISO 9002 and increased employee involvement in total quality efforts. At Pioneer, I had the opportunity to refine the techniques I had developed at Toro and further develop an excellent instruction team. Together we came up with techniques and insights into this type of training which I want to share with you in this book.

The rewards gained from implementing these programs have been many. The programs themselves had caused shifts in organizational systems that had to be dealt with. Training in each of the companies developed a presence that had not been there before. Most of all, providing the vehicle for adults to learn and helping them believe they can learn has been one of the most personally satisfying experiences of my consulting career. Many of the learners that qualify for Basic Skills for Total Quality (BSTQ) training have shut down their desire to learn in a class setting due to past experiences or lack of confidence. In many cases, they have been nonparticipants in decision making in our organizations and in our society. The BSTQ classes help them realize they can learn and they can contribute. This opens up a different world for them, in which they begin to feel empowered and involved. They have told us that in the BSTQ classes they learn how to participate with a group and to ask questions when they do not understand. Their commitment to company quality goals increases as communication is facilitated between management and hourly levels. In turn, managers begin to exhibit behaviors that demonstrate their commitment to employee empowerment.

The organizations that are the subject of the case studies in this book have contributed greatly to our California economy. They have willingly and unhesitatingly invested their resources in the development of their California workforce with a vision of the future which will require better educated, more empowered, and involved employees. They have truly illustrated their belief in the value of their human resources.

I have been privileged to be involved in the development and implementation of these two programs and with the people who have participated in them.

The core of this book was completed when we began the 1995 implementation of BSTQ at Toro. In this new implementation I had an opportunity to refine and verify the processes that are described in the following chapters. I found that the processes as described are quite helpful and when I did not follow my own advice, I had problems with the roll out of the training. This experience increases my confidence that the information offered here will be helpful to those of you who champion the idea of increasing the ability of your workforce to understand TQM, follow TQM principles, and participate in the continuous improvement of your product and your workplace.

This book is intended to be a practical, user-friendly guide for nonacademic professionals to use in the discovery, development, and implementation phases of a training program that will increase the basic skill competence of the workforce as it develops total quality management philosophy and skills. It describes an organizational effort to truly empower employees by helping them develop the basic skills they need to be full partners in the continuous improvement efforts.

Whatever your position in your organization, if you are reading this book and you have concerns about the basic skill level of your workforce, this manual will serve as a guide for you to successfully implement such a program. When I refer to "you," I refer to anyone who would champion such an educational program in an organization. This could be the quality manager, human resource manager, training manager, operations manager, or any combination thereof.

I hope this material will help the readers trade in old mental models of how basic skills education needs to be taught and evaluated in business. Just as the human mind, body, and spirit are connected, so are basic skills and total quality management skills. One effects the other, so we benefit by developing both rather than separating them.

ACKNOWLEDGMENTS

Many people have been part of the development of the successful programs cited in the case studies that follow. Included are all of the managers and supervisors who have given their input as the programs developed. These companies are healthy places to work. The commitment to employee empowerment through education continues today in these companies.

I want to thank all of the employees who participated and continue to participate in the classes. Their willingness to learn and improve themselves has been exciting and gratifying.

The instructors, especially Sarah Romo and Jean Christopher, provided excellence in the classroom on a daily basis throughout the life of these programs. We have learned a lot together about developing basic workplace skills for quality improvement.

Larry Kujovich, who was general manager of the Toro Irrigation Division when the need for BSTQ was identified, and Diane Zak, then director of Human Resources, set an example for supporting such a workplace education program as we began at Toro. The support continues today with Cap Hendrix as general manager, Lyle Elliott, director of Human Resources and Holly Wardrop, manager of Human Resources. At Pioneer Electronic Technologies, Inc. we had the constant support of Mr. Yashima and his highly capable administrative assistant, Miriam Simmel who translated all of our communication back and forth from English to Japanese.

Finally, I am grateful to my editor Cindy Tokumitsu of Quality Resources for her patience, encouragement, and gentle tenacity in working with me on this material.

INTRODUCTION

As the U.S. workplace has evolved over the years, the issues and challenges critical to competitive survival have changed. The most recent discussions revolve around building a workforce for the information age while battling the problems of inadequate literacy and the lack of basic workplace skills. Continuous learning, training investment, total quality management, reengineering and job redesign are all related issues that have grown in importance over the past few years and require the participation of workers who possess at least the most basic workplace skills.

Yet, many organizations still find themselves without any improvement in quality, productivity, or profits in spite of the millions of dollars they may spend on quality and reengineering programs. Often, it takes an unsuccessful attempt at quality improvement before an organization realizes that its workforce does not have the prerequisite skills to support a successful quality implementation program.

This kind of hindsight can begin a cycle of blame—an unproductive, quality-inhibiting practice—that breeds frustration with workers' performance among management, frustration among workers with management's communication and team-building skills, and overall skepticism of and in-house jokes about employee empowerment and participatory management principles and techniques. This cycle of blame can have, at worst, a crippling effect on quality efforts, or it can be a wake-up call for the company to undergo extensive skill assessment, training, and development at all levels to cultivate the basic skills required for the successful transition to a total quality management culture.

This book will outline a process for building quality and success into a TQM development program and enable companies to identify the gap between the existing skills of the workforce and the skills that a successful TQM implementation program requires.

BASIC SKILLS FOR TOTAL QUALITY

An effective Basic Skills for Total Quality (BSTQ) training program should:

1. Identify the skill requirements of the TQM program to be implemented.

2. Address the existing skill levels of all segments of the company's workforce.

3. Provide whatever training is required for employees to be successful in a TQM environment.

Therefore, we can begin to build these skills layer by layer, preparing the trainees for actual TQM training.

At this point, you're probably holding your forehead, lamenting the time all of this is going to take. And it will take some time. The good news however is that TQM need not be put on hold until all other training is completed. The core TQM concepts can be developed while basic skills classes are being instructed. Furthermore, TQM concepts can be woven into the BSTQ training through:

• Modeling of behaviors.

• Introduction and use of TQM-specific vocabulary and concepts.

• Living the TQM philosophy (walking the walk).

• Building the self-confidence of the workers.

• Improving communication and presentation skills.

• Teaching problem-solving and teamwork skills.

In BSTQ, learners use force field analysis, learn to construct and read graphs, describe steps in job processes, and to construct flowcharts. The concept of the internal customer is developed along with the skills of seeking and receiving feedback. These concepts need to be presented and developed over a period of time and can be cycled through the content over and over so the learning builds and is integrated with other ideas and behaviors.

For many, the skill deficiencies being focused on in this book will seem excruciatingly basic. It is difficult for the more educated people in business to comprehend the level of skill deficiencies that exist in much of today's workforce. Those who remain open to the possibility that basic skill deficiencies may exist in their companies may find information in the following chapters that will help them recognize their existence, discover their nature, and implement an effective solution.

The basic skills for total quality (BSTQ) approach differs from other approaches to basic skill development in that it is not separate from the organization's quality or reengineering implementation, but is an integral part of this implementation. In this process, basic skills training that is prerequisite to the success of TQM establishes a partnership with the TQM program. Recent participants in Toro's BSTQ training who then attended the Quality Education System (QES) class have indicated they would not have been able to understand QES concepts if they had not studied them first in BSTQ class. When partnered with TQM, BSTQ can be a tool to establish inclusion in TQM as opposed to exclusion by nurturing the partnership between BSTQ and the daily operations of the organization as it strives to achieve its business goals through total quality management.

When the partnership approach between BSTQ and the business is practiced, total quality concepts and attitudes can be developed by modeling, practicing, and clarifying them daily in the classroom. The vocabulary and terminology of TQM can be demystified, making it usable at a pace that allows workers to integrate it into their own vocabulary. Participants can be encouraged to clarify communication and ask questions they perhaps would be embarrassed to ask in regular team meetings due to lack of specific knowledge. In the BSTQ classroom, learners are allowed to work at their own pace and develop the appropriate behaviors and skills in a safe environment where no one evaluates them on how they sound or act. Each class is a learning team that can acquire skills in team membership while improving their reading and writing skills.

Partnering is aided further by locating the training room close to major company activities. Contrast this with basic skills training that is implemented by sending employees off site and hiring a high school instructor or a community college instructor to teach remedial math and reading. This approach separates the employees who need basic skills training from the rest of the company and fosters an atmosphere of exclusion. BSTQ also uses the class time to clarify and build on the language, activities, and written materials of the workplace. It establishes a partnership with the operations of the business to increase the skills, confidence, and competence levels of the workers. BSTQ can be valuable as a means of increasing the inclusion of any workforce that will participate in a TQM environment.

Table 1 compares the characteristics of Adult Basic Education (ABE) approach to implementing basic skills training and the characteristics of the BSTQ approach to basic skills training.

TABLE 1   Comparison of ABE and BSTQ Characteristics

Usual Adult Basic Education (ABE) Training	BSTQ Training
1. Instructor qualifications— • Credentialed. • Primary experience in an adult classroom. • Can develop daily lesson plans.	1. Instructor qualifications— • May or may not be credentialed. • Has understanding of business. • Experience in business with adults. • Can develop work-related examples and lessons.
2. Measurement— • Grade level system.	2. Measurement— • Identified work competencies.
3. Assessment— • Standardized. • Computer printout.	3. Assessment— • Preferably customized incorporating familiar materials and work situations. • Preferably hand scored to reduce participant anxiety.
4. Materials— • Published outside. • Generic.	4. Materials— • Developed by instruction team. • Based on work situations. • Use the language of the specific workplace.

(continued)

The information in this book was developed and summarized from programs designed and implemented for The Toro Company Irrigation Division in Riverside, CA and the Pioneer Electronics Technology, Inc. (PET) facilities in Chino and Pomona, CA. These programs were in constant implementation over a four-year period with Pioneer and are still in progress as of this writing. Toro is presently implementing a new phase of BSTQ which includes the members of the workforce not previously included in training.

The Toro Company, Worldwide Irrigation Division, is a division of The Toro Company of Minneapolis, Minnesota. Toro Irrigation is a leading manufacturer and distributor of irrigation sprinklers, with over 45 product lines comprising over 1,000 total products. These products range from do-it-yourself sprinklers

TABLE 1   Continued

Usual Adult Basic Education (ABE) Training	BSTQ Training
5. Curriculum— • Structured. • Focused on adult employability requirements. • Skills appropriate for grade level.	5. Curriculum— • Flexible. • Focus on specific organization's quality education requirements. • Skills appropriate for work and participation in next level of quality education. • Developed to include skill competencies required by work.
6. Evaluation— • Test of skill mastery. • Completion of course.	6. Evaluation— • Program manager responsible for constant feedback to and from all stakeholders through interviews, reviews, discussion, and reports. • Attendance. • Mastery of competencies. • Application to workplace behaviors. • Movement towards business goal achievement.

for home irrigation systems, to Network 8000, an advanced computerized irrigation system that can control the irrigation requirements of an entire city from a central location. Toro distributes products to these markets through a dealer network of over 300 outlets in the United States, Canada, Australia and Great Britain.

Pioneer Electronic Corporation, based in Tokyo, Japan employs over 14,000 people worldwide, of which Pioneer Electronics Technologies, Inc. is a United States subsidiary controlling two plants. The first of the two plants, which produced speakers and racks for stereo systems at Duarte, California, underwent a series of expansions before moving to Pomona, California in February of 1987. In August of 1988 PET expanded into the manufacturing of projection television sets with the opening of its plant in Chino, California. These facilities employ over 400 people. The production workers at Pomona have an average of 7 years experience with several having worked there for 14 years. This group of workers is made up of 95% nonnative English speakers. These are the workers who created the success of the Duarte plant resulting in expansion and the ultimate transfer of the facility to Pomona. They created this success without the ability to speak English but with great ability to produce speakers and get their jobs done through interaction with Spanish-speaking supervisors.

The catalysts for the training programs at both Toro and PET were corporate business goals that required the participation and involvement of employees as never before required. The Toro Company embarked on a total quality initiative based on Philip Crosby's Quality Education System and Pioneer Electronics Technology, Inc. targeted ISO 9002 certification as its immediate goal. PET management looked to the Japanese philosophy of kaizen and the 5S approach to organize the workplace and help achieve that goal. Leadership at both companies possessed the vision to identify the tremendous skill gap in workers that these goals made evident.

It is easy for managers to assume that employees come to work naturally equipped with adequate basic skills. But many employees hide their skill deficiencies because they have not been required to practice these skills on the job. In some cases, they have actually been trained *not* to use these skills.

In addition to an extensive vocabulary of its own, some of the skills required by total quality management are:

Learning Skills

- Generating and testing hypotheses.
- Unfreezing and reframing—the ability to let go of familiar assumptions and view situations in a different context.

Gathering Data

- Observing and documenting.
- Creating checklists.
- Writing descriptions.
- Displaying data (basic chart construction).

Analyzing Data

- Prioritizing goals.
- Identifying and listing steps in a process.
- Reading flowcharts.
- Constructing flowcharts.
- Sequencing and ordering activities.
- Theorizing; "What does it mean?".
- Interpreting data.
- Identifying similarities and differences.
- Identifying patterns and trends.
- Considering both sides of a problem.
- Identifying strengths and weaknesses.

Problem Solving, Continuous Measurable Improvement

- Identifying root causes.
- Selecting solutions and alternative solutions.
- Selecting areas of focus.
- Setting objectives.
- Initiating action planning.
- Evaluating results.

Communication

- Listening.
- Clarifying meanings and expectations.
- Confronting conflict.
- Expressing differences in opinion.
- Participating in dialogue.
- Presenting ideas in groups (presentation skills).

Working in Teams

- Identifying appropriate behavior in teamwork situations.
- Validating input of other team members.
- Planning for timely completion of assignments.
- Describing problem situations objectively.
- Brainstorming.
- Analyzing team processes.

Each of these skills may require knowledge that is not necessarily common in the workforce. Add to this the fact that many employees who are expected to participate in these activities cannot read, write, or compute adequately and the issue of basic skills training becomes urgent.

ISO 9002 certification, while it does not appear to require as many specific skills of the workforce as TQM, either documents an effective total quality management system or illuminates the necessity for one. In the latter case, the company that truly wants to achieve total quality begins to realize that a total quality environment will not be created without improved communication with the workforce. ISO 9000 certification is difficult to attain without the involvement of the workforce in company communication and certification efforts.

Organizational processes must be documented, preferably with the input of those who implement them. Superior supervisor and employee communication skills are required for eliciting input, documenting processes, and checking for clarification and validity. Some of the foundational skills that stand out as requirements here are:

Documentation

- Describing specific steps and behaviors in detail.
- Sequencing specific process steps.
- Using clear language versus technical or academic language.
- Reading and interpreting process charts, drawings, and schematics.

Communication

- Eliciting information and clarification from others (questioning, clarifying).
- Listening.
- Clarifying meaning, expectations.
- Confronting conflict.
- Expressing differences in opinion.
- Participating in dialogue.
- Presenting ideas in groups (presentation skills).

Working in Teams

- Identifying appropriate behavior in team work situations.
- Validating input of other team members.
- Planning for timely completion of assignments.
- Describing problem situations objectively.
- Brainstorming.
- Analyzing team processes.

The identification of either of these long-term organizational goals, coupled with a realistic assessment of existing employee skill levels, allows the organization to identify the skill gap which must be narrowed in order for these long-term goals to be achieved.

Summary of Important Points

- Changes in the U.S. workplace have made basic skills, especially learning skills, necessary for the frontline worker.

- Basic skills and basic total quality skills can be taught at the same time.

- ISO 9000 certification requires employees to have at least a minimum of basic English language skills.

DISCOVERY

DECIDE TO BEGIN

Step 1: Decide to Begin

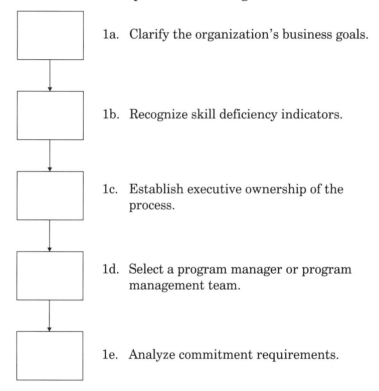

1a. Clarify the organization's business goals.

1b. Recognize skill deficiency indicators.

1c. Establish executive ownership of the process.

1d. Select a program manager or program management team.

1e. Analyze commitment requirements.

Phase I—Discovery Process

The first step in the Discovery Phase, part of the three-phase process of Basic Skills for Total Quality, is Decide to Begin. This step consists of the above five interconnected parts.

A brief look backward into the history of organizational management tells us how the current drought in basic functional workplace skills came about. The numerous theories that shaped traditional management theory evolved into a set of concepts that included hierarchical structure, span of control, management by exception, specialization by function, line-staff dichotomy, and management responsibility for monitoring and controlling. Management stars excelled at "fire fighting" and were rewarded for the ability to quickly react in a crisis. Early management concepts emphasized increased efficiency through control of the workers and attention to production and sales numbers.

Information was provided, if at all, to employees on an as-needed basis controlled and disseminated by top management. Employee participation and involvement were not goals of most companies in the United States until the quality movement of the 1980s and early 1990s. Until then, patriarchal "father-knows-best" management styles were the style of the day and the ideal employee showed up, asked few questions, and did what they were told. Communication and team-building training dollars were spent on mid- to upper-level management. Hourly workers typically received only the technical training required to do their job faster and improve efficiency, if they received any training at all.

CHANGE FOR THE FUTURE

The first foray into quality circles in the 1970s was less than successful for many companies. That there would need to be organizational change and supportive management behaviors that valued employee involvement in process improvement was not a widespread concept.

Organizations began to see that massive changes in the way that work was performed, managed, and marketed must take place to compete in the marketplace of the 1990s. Having learned from the failures, in many instances, of quality circles, organizations embraced the concept of total quality management, which had been instrumental in assisting Japan improve its reputation for producing quality products.

Total quality management, an umbrella term that describes the many quality improvement programs that have spread through the United States in the past three decades, requires the involvement of every employee in problem-solving and quality improvement efforts.

A new wave of total quality cultural change has been attempted in many cases with a workforce that remember all too well earlier failed quality circle attempts. They have seen management fads come and go without making any apparent improvements or changes in management behavior. Many workforce populations still survive in an environment where they are given inadequate information and are rewarded for production numbers or sales quotas with little attention paid to process or customer satisfaction. In many organizations, TQM is still a hard sell resulting in resistance to change and behaviors that contradict the organization's quality vision. Even though the slogans have been memorized and new jargon has been learned, actually empowering employees is much more complicated and essential to TQM success.

EMPOWERING EMPLOYEES FOR SUCCESS

An important part of empowering employees is providing them with the skills they need to be competent and successful with their new level of participation. It is not enough to give them new responsibilities; this will only frustrate them. Empowerment will not be achieved or seen as an effective method of managing the workplace without some skills training.

The primary motivation that drives Basic Skills for Total Quality training is the organization's intention of empowering employees to improve quality and, ultimately, profitability. The successful approach to empowerment is to identify the employees' training needs and implement corresponding training so they can succeed in the new workplace environment. When this approach is taken, employees and the organization can share the benefits of true empowerment.

Therefore, Basic Skills for Total Quality is a process for providing employees with the skills for successful empowerment. BSTQ occurs in three interwoven phases, each with several steps.

Phase I: Discovery

Discovery means identifying the skills that employees of an organization need to participate in a quality or reengineering initiative. Discovery consists of four steps:

1. Decide to begin.
2. Clarify internal customer requirements and expectations.
3. Discover perceptions of current skill levels.
4. Assess basic skills of the workforce.

Phase II: Development

Development means developing curricula and materials that are work related and customized for the individual company. Development consists of three steps:

1. Select and develop an instruction team.
2. Identify the curriculum and competencies and establish a tracking system.
3. Develop the curriculum and materials.

Phase III: Implementation

Implementation means implementing a BSTQ training program that models total quality improvement, involves the customers, and provides continuous feedback and evaluation. Implementation consists of three steps:

1. Communicate with internal customers.
2. Seek continuous feedback and evaluation.
3. Celebrate success.

Figure 1.1 illustrates the three phases of a BSTQ program and how the steps in each phase form a whole and also connect the other phases. Each step adds to the body of knowledge involved in BSTQ program development and implementation.

Figure 1.2 is a process flowchart that shows how specific actions are connected as BSTQ is implemented.

1A. CLARIFY THE ORGANIZATION'S BUSINESS GOALS

It is critical that organizations develop their vision of what they will become to achieve success in the future. Most companies'

Three Major Phases of a BSTQ Program

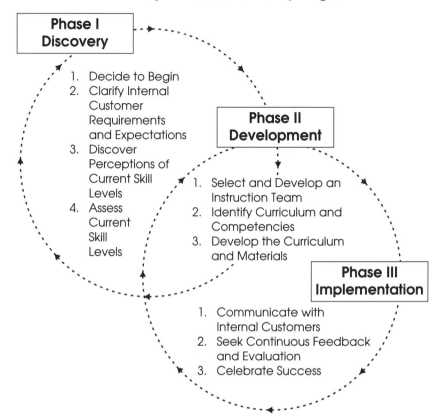

FIGURE 1.1. **Basic Skills for Total Equality.**

vision statements now include a dedication to total quality improvement either directly or indirectly. When this type of organizational goal exists, planning for functional areas, including training, can have a clearer focus.

Once there is a clear organizational business goal, individual divisions and departments can use it as a guide with which they align their own objectives and goals. This view of what the organization must become in order to compete allows each part of the organization to describe its role in the new organization and compare it to its current role.

The realization that goals cannot be reached by continuing to do the same things with the current workforce, equipped with its

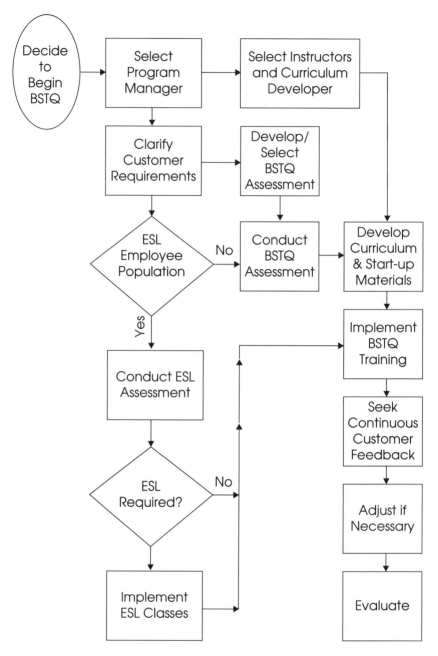

FIGURE 1.2. **Development and Implementation of a BSTQ Training Program.**

current skills, comes at different points in total quality management implementation. Progressive companies realize this up front while others wait until TQM fails. The latter is an expensive way to go and surely delays company goal achievement. The trouble with afterthought training is that the quality effort gets a bad reputation due to failure and resulting negative mindsets.

How to determine business goals is outside the scope of this book, and numerous excellent resources are available to help with this step. The step, however, is a foundation for effective quality training, including basic skills.

1B. RECOGNIZE SKILL DEFICIENCY INDICATORS

It is important for managers, supervisors, quality professionals, and others to recognize the signs that skill deficiencies exist. This is done most readily by observing and listening to communication. Supervisors may feel frustration with employee motivation or commitment. Employees may express feelings of inadequacy, confusion, or anger over interactions with supervisors. It is important to realize that the first signs of basic skill deficiencies may surface as attitude problems, lack of commitment, and production problems.

A common indication of skill deficiencies is frequent supervisor comments regarding frustrations with the workers. This may actually reveal two levels of inadequate basic skills in frontline workers and supervisors:

1. Lack of basic skills for total quality (BSTQ) training.

2. Lack of supervisory skill.

The following list of indicators can be used in investigating the possibility of existing skill deficiencies:

- Rework, waste.

- Lack of communication in English.

- Inability to follow work instructions (oral or written).

- Employees covering up for each other.

- Lack of commitment to quality.
- Supervisor assumptions that workers are incompetent or slow to learn.
- Lack of acceptance of responsibility.
- Lack of self-confidence.
- Absence of initiative or lack of participation.
- Inaccurate or no reading of work instructions.
- Errors in paperwork.
- Few written suggestions.

Some indicators of inadequate supervisory skills as related to basic workplace skills are:

- Constant frustration with employee performance.
- Frustration with employee commitment.
- All of the indicators of BSTQ skill deficiencies.

These indicators could lead to the discovery of skill deficiencies other than BSTQ, but they definitely flag the need to investigate the underlying causes of these skill deficiencies. While investigating causes, be aware of the possibility that the employees and supervisors involved have not developed basic skills that will allow them to actively participate in quality improvement training and efforts.

1C. ESTABLISH EXECUTIVE OWNERSHIP OF THE PROCESS

The decision to begin a BSTQ program ideally comes from the CEO or other top company executive. The request for a discovery process may come from other concerned individuals, but the decision to begin must have the support of the CEO and other executives when possible. Getting started can be accomplished without this support, but maintaining a program and completing it successfully requires commitment from the top. For instance, in long-term programs, there will always come a point at which immediate production pressures outweigh perceived long-term benefits of training. It is critical at this point that the top exccutives back the training in order to successfully continue the program. Getting senior executive commitment is less difficult today than it was in the past because today most senior executives understand the importance and benefits of training the workforce.

In order to secure executive buy in, you will need to present your case for Basic Skills for Total Quality to him or her. Do your homework on the type of presentation that appeals to this executive and make sure you have data, visuals, and cost/benefit analysis prepared. There are also video presentations available through the National Alliance of Business and published studies available from the American Society for Training and Development. If you are going to use a consultant, have this individual present their qualifications to the senior executive.

If the decision to begin a discovery process is initiated by someone other than the senior executive, the idea eventually will have to be sold to other decision makers including the senior executive to ensure the program's success.

1D. SELECT A PROGRAM MANAGER OR PROGRAM MANAGEMENT TEAM

It is important to select a program manager or management team almost simultaneously with the decision to begin a skills discovery process. This person can organize the discovery process and present the information to the rest of the company. It is important to select a dedicated and skillful program manager or management team with internal contacts and credibility, excellent consulting skills, training and development experience, and knowledge of quality concepts. This person or team could be an external consultant, an internal consultant, or a partnership of the two leading a small team. The advantages of this partnership are the combined strengths of both an external and an internal person. While I believe this model is the most effective, it may not always be possible.

The benefits of an externally selected program manager are that an external person can focus on this program specifically rather than concentrating on other issues in the organization that may arise and cause a distraction. This person can have skills which are more focused on program development and management, and if the external person does not manage the program effectively, he or she is easier to replace than an internal person.

If an internal person is assigned as the program manager, the knowledge of the informal network as a way of accomplishing tasks and spreading information will be helpful. Also, the understanding of and dedication to the business goals of the organization can be useful. The downside of assigning an internal person to this role is that other responsibilities within the organization may take precedence. At any moment one of these other responsibilities can become more important and the BSTQ program will have to slide for a short period of time.

A program manager will be required full time in the beginning of the development and implementation of this program.

Duties of the Program Manager

The duties of the program manager require many skills but especially consulting and diplomacy skills. This person will keep the program focused and on target while managing the organization's perceptions of the training. The program manager's main role will be to ensure the success of the program in the eyes of the organization. This will involve balancing concerns of participants, supervisors, management, and instructors so that expectations and needs are met while achieving a mastery of competencies. The program manager should have exceptional counseling and communication skills along with a background knowledge of and experience with total quality management. This knowledge should show in the approach to the customers, managers, supervisors, participants, and other employees. The program manager must be able to demonstrate problem solving in daily interactions and, most importantly, must be positive and believe in the ability of the participants to learn.

Table 2 outlines the skills and knowledge required by the multiple roles of the program manager. The duties of the program manager will be further discussed in chapter 5 as we begin to discuss program development.

Table 2 shows the variety of skills and knowledge that the BSTQ program manager will need.

TABLE 2   Program Manager Selection

Roles	Skills and Knowledge
Keep training focused and on target.	Planning; use management tools.
Manage the training logistics.	Scheduling. Long-range planning. Balancing organizational resources. Be flexible yet maintain focus.
Manage the organization's perceptions and training.	Systems thinking. Positive attitude. Communication, conflict management. Public relations skills.
Coordinate concepts, vocabulary and practices with total quality management.	Knowledge of TQM and curriculum design.
Support and develop instructors for continuous measurable improvement.	Train-the-Trainer skills. People development skills. Ability to give specific feedback. Problem-solving skills.
Manage conflicts and solve problems.	Understand prolem-solving model of TQM. Confront issues without antagonizing personalities. Strive for continuous improvement.

With the project manager or project management team in place, BSTQ can begin with Phase I: Discovery. As this task is carried out, gaps in skills can be identified through interaction with management, human resources staff, or other members of the organization who are responsible for the success of the company's business goals. These gaps identify training and development opportunities that exist and allow the organization to align training objectives with the department goals.

1E. ANALYZE COMMITMENT REQUIREMENTS

The BSTQ process will require substantial commitments of time, money, facilities, and faith. Recommendations for these elements should be provided in a proposal to the decision makers. Because these commitments are extensive, they should be described and compared to the costs of *not* training. Usually training is clearly the better decision. These costs should never be underestimated; if costs are estimated accurately, or even generously, any future cost-related surprises can be minimized. This will buy some program insurance. Keeping an eye on the long-term implementation of such a program is essential to success.

The following is an overview of three important elements to be covered in the proposal to implement a BSTQ program:

- Time requirements.
- Facility requirements.
- Financial resource requirements.

Time Requirements

The successful implementation of both the Toro Company program and the PET program can be attributed in part to the fact that each was completed on company time. The employees that are involved in this type of program usually work as many hours as they are allowed to, including overtime, if available. After work they have many personal responsibilities that make putting in extra class hours stressful. There will likely come a time when these employees have enough confidence in their ability to learn that they will choose to spend some of their personal time improving their skills and knowledge base. However, until their self-confidence is increased by having successful learning experiences, it is much more effective to train them on company time. It will be seen as a definite benefit by employees and as a vote of confidence in their abilities and value, and the return on company investment will be substantial.

In order to implement an extensive BSTQ training program, management must make a firm commitment to allow a reasonable percent of the workforce to be in training at a given time.

This percentage should be kept below 10 percent and preferably no more than 7 percent of the workforce at any one time. This commitment can be realized with additional coverage such as temporary or cross trained personnel for peak production or service hours. At both case study sites, for example, other employees covered for the people attending the training. This required supervisors to plan ahead for line coverage. Sometimes this also required temporary workers to cover production needs.

Even with dedicated funds for temporary personnel, constant training will begin to pinch production. There is one thing of which you can be absolutely sure—despite the numbers you agree to on paper, when the training participants leave the front lines it will be a shock to the supervisor in charge. Making that first mass exodus of employees as painless as possible will be important as the program progresses and is an important role of the program manager.

Facility Requirements

The second important commitment that must be made involves dedicating the necessary rooms and equipment to training. This includes the promise that the room and its equipment will not be used by anyone else in the company for consistently scheduled periods of time for the duration of the program. It is also important to have an adequate system in place for scheduling such rooms and equipment.

If this commitment is not honored, the training program will begin to deteriorate. Each time the training sessions are moved to another room, or equipment is borrowed and not returned, lack of respect for the training program is communicated. On the other hand, the program manager can make other arrangements for class once in a while when special circumstances require. In this, as in most instances, communication, mutual respect, and cooperation will make the changes work.

Many companies do not have enough meeting space to accommodate the new emphasis on teams that is a part of any total quality program. They quickly find that the nice room down the hall that has always been underutilized is now constantly in use. So setting rooms aside for training, which have always been available for other purposes, requires cooperation from the entire organization.

As the case study examples will illustrate, getting a commitment for a dedicated training room is sometimes difficult. In long-term training programs, this commitment may have to be renegotiated several times.

Financial Resource Requirements

Needless to say, ongoing, long-term training is expensive. Employee time charged to indirect labor and temporary personnel coverage are all aspects of training that add to the cost. Realistically assessing the costs of such a program is important. Getting the best return on this investment is critical.

THE TORO COMPANY

The Toro Company, Irrigation Division in Riverside, California had been informed in early 1990 by the corporate office in Minneapolis that the entire company would be implementing the Crosby Total Quality Education program with the specific goals of implementing total quality improvement processes and implementing cross functional teams as a means of achieving zero defects.

The signs that the hourly workforce at the Riverside division of Toro did not have the skills to participate in cross functional teams or Crosby Quality training were recognized before total quality implementation began. Toro's human resource department realized there was a basic skills problem when they requested that new health forms be filled out in a meeting. It previously had been common practice for employees to take such forms home, fill them out, and return them. This provided employees with the opportunity to have other household members complete the forms for them and hide their inadequate basic skills. When asked to complete the forms in the meeting, several of the forms came back with identical answers in the blanks. The workers in question had simply copied from each other. Another indicator of basic skill deficiency was the speaking of native languages other than English on the line leading to the assumption that English skills were lacking.

In addition, statistical process control (SPC) training of 10 hours per employee had been completed and determined to be successful. Later it became obvious that this SPC training was failing to increase SPC involvement and capability on the floor.

A possible explanation for the misperceived success of SPC training is that the learners were able to memorize enough information by rote so that they appeared to be grasping the concepts. These trainees were mostly Asian and Hispanic females, not likely to speak up or admit they did not understand. Their typical response was to nod their head. The inexperienced instructor with a technical background did not realize that this seemingly affirmative response did not indicate understanding. However, this instructor was knowledgeable and did the best he could with no Train-the-Trainer experience or knowledge of the cultural issues or the level of basic skill involved.

The criteria unofficially used to evaluate the first SPC training were:

- Attendance.

- Positive learner attitudes.

- Accurate responses on classroom content evaluation.

After the training, management realized that the employees who participated were not able to apply the SPC skills in the workplace. Possible reasons for this are that the participants lacked the prerequisite skills for SPC training and a lack of guided follow-up and application of SPC on the manufacturing floor.

A general perception of Toro Irrigation's management was that communication was poor and language skills were inadequate for further participation in quality training. This perception, along with the inability to apply SPC after 10 hours of training, suggested to them that perhaps the hourly workforce did in fact lack the skills to participate in and contribute to the quality initiative overall.

At Toro, the average length of employment was 12 years with several workers having tenure of 18 years. Never in that time had the hourly workforce received any formal training except for the recent 10-hour course in statistical process control. The quality initiative was going to require very different skills and behaviors from everyone, especially the hourly workers.

The first request for information regarding a possible discovery process came from the director of human resources who had been with the company for several years and was very familiar with the skill level of the workforce. She had full support of the general manager in this project so there was never any question of project ownership.

I was brought in as program manager at the very beginning of the Discovery phase. The team consisted of the Human Resources staff and myself. Manufacturing personnel were consulted regularly for guidance in curriculum development and implementation.

There was a great deal of discussion regarding when the training should take place, whether half could be on company time and half on employee time, all on employee time, or all on company time. After looking at many aspects of this question, the program management team decided that the most effective approach would be to offer all of the BSTQ training on company time. This proved to be not only an effective approach, but also a great morale booster for the trainees. Employees covered positions for each other while others went to class. Some temporary workers were hired to cover positions left vacant due to training.

In the beginning, facilities were a problem at Toro. However, using a creative, positive, "can do" approach to problem solving, some undeveloped storage space was discovered, and with some assistance from the company maintenance crew, it was transformed into an unexpectedly adequate training room. This room quickly became attractive for other meetings, and attention was required for scheduling. After a few months, this area was involved in a human resource department conversion, so another area was renovated in the engineering department. This room was used for a while until engineering began to watch it covetously, and scheduling again became an issue. Finally, the human resource department reconstruction was completed and a dedicated training room was established.

PIONEER ELECTRONICS TECHNOLOGY, INC. (PET)

The signs that basic skill gaps existed at Pioneer Electronics Technology, Inc. in Pomona and Chino were apparent to the management personnel responsible for achieving ISO 9002 certification. The primary indicator at PET was English language deficiency in both the hourly worker group and the supervisor group.

Although ISO 9000 certification can be obtained without an English speaking workforce, PET's management decided to target better education, learning skills, and improved communication skills for its workforce with a view toward long-term benefits. They expected the concepts of Kaizen (incremental improvements to achieve higher standards) to be implemented in the workplace along with the 5S's of workplace organization. In most cases, peeling back the layer of English language skill deficiency provided the freedom to work on the other basic skills.

Well-known in the electronics industry, Pioneer's facility in Pomona has a loyal workforce that is 95 percent Hispanic and has an average tenure of 7 to 8 years with several employees there 14 years. The majority of communication in the past with this non-English-speaking workforce was through Spanish-speaking supervisors and personnel department workers and a company newsletter written in both English and Spanish. Much of this workforce had never had the opportunity to go to school in the United States, and many of them had little schooling in their native country. Before the requirements of employee involvement and documentation of processes, these employees functioned well with the skills they had.

However, now their jobs were changing at every level, and it was apparent to management that a common language was needed in order for all levels of the organization to improve communication with each other. It also became clear that computation, problem-solving, and analytical skills were going to be increasingly important at the supervisory level.

Pioneer Electronics Technology is a Japanese-owned company and the managers at both the Chino and the Pomona plant were Japanese nationals. The request for the training came from the Japanese president of PET and was totally supported by him throughout the life of the training program. He committed funds for temporaries to cover the production workload and never wavered from his goal of educating the workforce.

Again, I was brought in early in the planning for the discovery process. The personnel department worked with me to plan the discovery and implementation phases of the project.

Here too, the suggestion was made that employees could participate in the training partly on their own time. However, Pioneer worked 10-hour days, four days per week so there was not much time left for attending class. According to their comments, the employees appreciated being able to attend on company time. They saw this as a real benefit for them and they applied themselves to the learning task. Positions which were vacated by trainees for four hours per week during the training were covered by temporary employees on a rotating basis. While this gesture provided adequate coverage of manufacturing tasks, the additional employees impacted the supervisors' efficiency report.

At Pioneer, one facility dedicated two conference rooms to training for one and a half years, and the other facility used one conference room constantly for two years. At times they used two rooms, and for one session, used part of the cafeteria.

These firm commitments to the program by the president and managers at PET set the stage in the beginning for successful implementation of BSTQ training. These commitments included training on company time, allocating funds for hiring temporary employees to cover positions vacated by training participants, and dedicating conference rooms to the training on a regular basis. These commitments by PET communicated to employees that the training was important to the company.

SUMMARY OF IMPORTANT POINTS

1. Organizational total quality management goals may create a gap between skills required for participation in TQM and existing skills.

2. ISO 9000 certification efforts may create a gap between required skills and existing skills.

3. Nonnative speakers of English may need English-as-a-Second-Language instruction before they participate in BSTQ.

4. A highly skilled program manager should be selected as soon as the decision to begin is made.

5. Commitment to training of time, facilities, and financial resources will show organizational support.

CLARIFY INTERNAL CUSTOMER REQUIREMENTS AND EXPECTATIONS

Step 2: Clarify Internal Customer Requirements
and Expectations

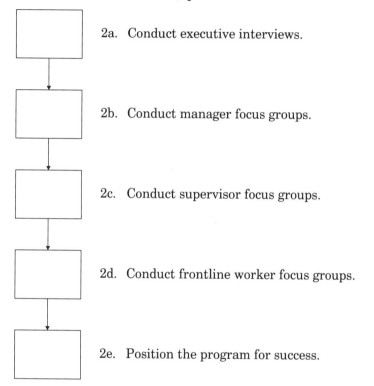

2a. Conduct executive interviews.

2b. Conduct manager focus groups.

2c. Conduct supervisor focus groups.

2d. Conduct frontline worker focus groups.

2e. Position the program for success.

Phase I—Discovery Process

The second step of Phase I, Clarify Internal Customer Requirements and Expectations, consists of the above five parts.

The purpose of this step is to clarify the expectations of all the internal customers of the BSTQ training. This allows the internal customers to verbalize expectations of the training and set some priorities for the way the instructional time will be spent. It is a time of accepting ownership, collaborating on curriculum identification, and clarifying expectations of the training.

TABLE 3 Discovery Phase Interviews and Focus Groups

Level	Structure	Length/ Number	Format
Executive	Interviews	30 to 45 minutes	One on one
Middle management	Focus groups and/or interviews	1 hour; focus group to include critical managers	6 to 9 participants; facilitated by program manager
Supervisors and leads	Focus groups	1 hour; repeat to include all supervisors	6–9 participants; facilitated by program manager
Frontline workers	Focus groups	1 hour; repeat to ensure representation from all areas participating in assessment and training	6–9 employees; facilitated by program manager

Every level of the organization should be included in the initial data gathering of the discovery phase. The main structure for this initial data gathering is a combination of interviews and focus groups. Table 3 provides information regarding the recommended length and size of these meetings. The number of meetings depends on the size of the management staff and the size of the workforce. It is better to have too many information gathering meetings than too few. The data may not change, but more people will be involved and accept ownership of the program.

2A. CONDUCT EXECUTIVE INTERVIEWS

All executives who will eventually evaluate the training program should be interviewed in the discovery phase. This interview allows the program manager to identify the expectations and concerns of each individual on the executive team. It also allows the program manager to establish credibility, build rapport, and position him or herself as a team player in the total quality initiative. Possible questions to be asked or requests for information to be made might include the following:

- Describe what will be happening in your organization when your business goals are being met or when total quality management is successfully implemented.
- How is that different from what is happening now?
- What do employees need to do differently before the organization can achieve its business goals?
- What will they be doing that they have not been asked to do before?
- Do you see the hiring requirements changing in the future? If so, why?

Often, executives who do not seem to be involved with the Basic Skills for Total Quality training in the beginning will be called upon to decide on budgetary priorities or to recommend the continuation of programs in the months to come. It is good preventive planning to involve everyone in the discovery phase who will be aware of the BSTQ implementation. It is better to give too many people too much information than to be viewed as withholding information from people who should be fully informed and committed. As in other total quality management processes, those who are involved up front are much more likely to be supportive through the end of the implementation. In other words, it is important to create ownership of the program among the executives.

Executive interviews are the first step in positioning BSTQ training as one level of training required for total quality management. As the program manager asks and the executives answer questions regarding new skills that will be required by different groups in the organization, the stage will be set for emphasizing that this is just one type of training among several that will be implemented. Successful TQM begins with executive and management development in TQM principles and tools. Then, supervisors learn new ways of monitoring processes and interacting with their staff, employees are organized into different work group configurations, and team training begins. As new vocabulary begins to slip into everyday work conversations, the timing is perfect to position BSTQ training as part of the workforce training for TQM implementation.

Spending time in interviews to obtain executive input, even from executives who are not directly involved with the program, will be effective public relations for the phases of the program yet to come. Attending to public relations within the company is an important part of creating any successful, long-term program. This is part of the process of satisfying internal customers, and it begins to model an important element of the TQM environment.

After the interviews and focus groups, the data should be summarized and provided to the executives and focus groups for any revisions or additions. If you have enough lead time, it is preferable to give the executives the summary before you present it to the entire group that participated.

2B. CONDUCT MANAGER FOCUS GROUPS

Manager focus groups are important in order to accomplish the following:

- Identify management goals for the training effort.
- Clarify the expectations for the training.
- Get management involved in planning the training program.
- Address the concerns of management.
- Communicate the importance of management support for the ongoing training.
- Describe behaviors that show support for the training.

As organizations begin to flatten out, the middle management group loses clear definition. The best advice with this group is to err on the side of too much involvement rather than not enough. Certainly, any managers who will work directly with supervisors during the implementation of training should be included in the focus groups. Their support will be important as the training is rolled out and implementation is maintained. Even though they are not typically involved in the program development activities and not directly impacted by the absence of employees attending training, they must be aware of the program's progress. Often, members of this group have been responsible for some type of training in the company and appreciate having their experience in this area recognized. They can be an excellent source of information.

These managers also will need to provide resource support for adequate floor and production coverage when needed. This coverage should be included in the budget as part of the cost of training. If managers begin to feel a budget pinch that could keep them from meeting production or service goals due to inadequate numbers of personnel, the program will be severely impacted. If funds are designated for adequately covering the lines during training, it will be easier to resist the urge to improve the profit picture by not hiring the designated backup personnel.

Focus groups begin with an executive introducing the program manager who explains the proposed training program. As described in the executive interviews, the proposed training is positioned as part of the companywide training for total quality management in which everyone will participate.

Next, the flow of the program is introduced with a brief explanation of the three phases of implementation and a general description of how the program will roll out. Then the meeting moves into its main purpose which is to gather data (Table 4 shows an example of an agenda for such a focus group.)

You can conduct this data gathering effort by using a simple structure that can be used for each of the subsequent focus groups with some minor customization of each. The format consists of the following three questions:

1. What would you like your employees to do better?

2. What would you like to do better?

3. What would you like your manager to do better?

These three questions elicit a great deal of data which is invaluable when the competencies are being identified.

TABLE 4 Focus meeting agenda

1. Introduction to Basic Skills for Total Quality program plans.
   * Introduction of program manager.
   * Explanation of need for this program.
   * Need for input.
2. Flow of BSTQ
   * Discovery phase (assessment).
   * Development phase.
   * Implementation phase.
   * Ongoing evaluation and customer feedback.
3. Data gathering.
   * Description of current data gathering methods.
   * Individual data input.
4. Next steps.

2C. CONDUCT SUPERVISOR FOCUS GROUPS

The supervisor group is important because they are the individuals whose work will be greatly impacted on a daily basis for many months. It is critical that they be supportive, take ownership, and participate in the identification of job skills and curriculum development.

Supervisor focus groups are an excellent opportunity to accomplish the following:

* Obtain supervisor buy in.

* Identify and address concerns.

* Gather data.

* Clarify expectations.

* Communicate the importance of manager and supervisor support and positive attitude regarding the training.

* Describe behaviors that show support for the training.

* Position the BSTQ training as one part of a total quality management initiative.

* Identify methods of informal evaluation.

- Describe changes in behavior that supervisors will expect to see as a result of the training.

If a supervisor has a history of resisting program implementation or change, that person should be included in this group. It will be easier to be positive about a program an individual helps develop.

Often, the supervisors in a company have varying abilities themselves. Some of these supervisors will have worked for the company for many years, being promoted to supervisor because they could do the job very well. It is possible that a few of these supervisors have inadequate reading, writing, and math skills. If so, their survival secret has probably depended upon them being able to get someone else to do the tasks that they could not do (e.g., write a memo or read the process sheet to another employee.)

TQM may require supervisors to use different skills than the job has previously required. It is not easy for any individual to hide inadequate reading, writing, or computation skills in a TQM training class or in a team meeting. The new methods of planning and conducting the work may require them to record data on a flip chart or figure averages and efficiencies as part of a team. These new methods may also require them to serve on cross functional teams with upper management personnel. In order to be effective team members, they will need to be confident in their abilities to participate on an equal level with the rest of the team.

Because the professional rank between frontline worker and lead or supervisor is not great, it is common for a BSTQ training program to produce some anxiety on the part of leads and supervisors who are a little insecure about their own skills. This type of training (which was almost never done in the past) brings up all kinds of feelings of inadequacy in the lead or supervisor group. This is especially true if the lead or supervisor isn't clear about the total quality management initiative and where he or she will fit in to the new company culture. It is difficult to see the people you supervise being taught concepts and skills you may not know or have. Therefore, care and nurturing of the lead or supervisor group is critical to program success.

Supervisors will probably interact with the participants of the BSTQ training more than any other management personnel, so their perception of the training is exceptionally important. Focus groups that include supervisors and informal interviews, which will be discussed later, allow the program manager to identify methods of informal evaluation that will be used by supervisors. In other words, what behaviors will they really expect to see?

2D. CONDUCT FRONTLINE WORKER FOCUS GROUPS

The focus group meeting of frontline workers can be one of the most important groups for gathering and disseminating information. The individuals in this group should be chosen for their informal leadership abilities as much as possible. By the time this group meets, they will have already formed opinions about the impending assessment and training. Therefore, it will be critical that the correct information be available to them. This meeting can follow the same agenda as the management focus group meetings. The same three questions posed to the supervisor and manager groups should be asked, with some modification.

The answers to these questions will help to do the following:

• Identify the benefits of the training.

• Reassure workers of the purpose of the classes and that there will be no grades or homework.

• Position the assessment as a way to assure that the classes will be presented at the right difficulty level for the participants.

• Feed the informal information network accurate, positive information about the training.

Each focus group meeting with frontline workers will include them in the planning and discovery process to greater degree. Lots of accurate information about the discovery process and resulting training will minimize negative rumors. The focus group meeting also serves to build rapport between the program manager and the frontline workers. After the meeting, when the program manager visits the manufacturing floor, there will be familiar faces, smiles, and names that can be applied to faces to further build trust and good will. The focus group will be a great help in breaking down any resistance and increase the acceptance of the training to come. At this point, all levels of the organization will have provided input for the training program.

Participation in focus groups should be documented and reported in a summary of the data. This record keeping helps employees remember they were part of the development process. It also allows the program manager to ensure as nearly as possible that all critical personnel have at least been asked to provide input and direction.

2E. POSITION THE PROGRAM FOR SUCCESS

The last part of Step 2, Position the Program for Success, enables the program manager to position the assessment and the training in a way that is most advantageous to the success of the program. Comments about the planned training program that help to position it positively can be interjected into formal and informal meetings and can be used to answer individual concerns. These comments include the following:

- The total quality management culture and the business goals it supports require everyone in the company to acquire new skills. Some employees will require training in basic skills in order to participate in TQM training and contribute to organizational business goals.

- The BSTQ program will be a company's investment in people it values.

- The training will be a review of skills employees may have had at one time but have not used in years.

- The training program will be a way for employees to make the transition back into a classroom setting after years of being out of school.

- There will be no grades.

- These are the same good employees that have always worked for the company as it became successful. Their jobs are changing with total quality management and ex-

WORKSHEET:
ASSESSING SKILL REQUIREMENTS OF EMPLOYEES

Manager, Supervisor

Beneath each of the questions below, list as specifically as possible the skills and behaviors appropriate to each category.

1. What would you like your employees to learn or do better in order to implement total quality management?

2. What would you like to learn or do better in order to implement total quality management?

3. What would you like your manager to learn or do better in order to implement total quality management?

Frontline Workers

Depending on the existing stage of TQM implementation, these questions may have to leave out referral to TQM. Beneath each of the questions below, list as specifically as possible the skills and behaviors appropriate to each category.

1. What would you like other employees to learn or do better in order to implement total quality management?

2. What would you like to learn or do better in order to implement total quality management?

3. What would you like your supervisor to learn or do better in order to implement total quality management?

pectations of their performance will be changing. It is important to develop these skills so employees can be successful in the new environment.

Addressing Workforce Concerns

An important part of any successful training program roll out is the care and nurturing of the social impact on the workforce. The focus groups provide a way to get the word out in a positive way, with representatives of their own groups spreading positive perceptions and truthful facts.

In order to deflect the apprehension in the workforce, both the supervisor focus groups and the frontline worker focus groups need to be very clear on the following points that address the fear level of the employee population:

1. **What will happen to employees as a result of the assessment scores?** Nothing happens. If their basic skills are lower than they need to be, it only indicates what the training program needs to do for them. If they do well, nothing happens.

   We made this comment over and over at Toro and at Pioneer to point out that the purpose of the assessment was to discover what the training program needed to do for the employees. This helped to allay fears, but nothing except experience could completely get rid of deep-seated insecurities of not measuring up.

2. **What will happen to the scores themselves? Where will they be kept? Who will have access to them?** Scores should be kept in a training data base, separate from the personnel records. It is helpful to have an external person responsible for scores, as this reassures the employees that the information will be kept truly separate from their personnel file. It is also important that someone remember this promise when requests are made by supervisors for information about a worker's classroom performance. Complete trust in this area takes time and behavioral proof. Human resource and training and development professionals usually observe ethical standards which include not reporting the content of training sessions to management unless the participant requests that

intervention. It is hoped that as manufacturing personnel perform more and more of their own training, they continue to maintain standards that protect the autonomy of individuals so that the training session can continue to be a supportive, nonthreatening environment.

3. **Will attending a Basic Skills for Total Quality class be mandatory?** This particular training seems to be most effective when it is voluntary, meaning the employee can refuse the opportunity to attend class. It is important, however, that employees understand that the training is preparing them to fully participate in more training sessions and the total quality culture. To participate can be their choice as long as they understand the company's business goals and how they may need to upgrade their skills.

In long-term programs where over 100 employees are identified for BSTQ training, there will be plenty of time for the dissenters to change their minds. The first classes that go through training will be the best advertising for the program provided it has the right curriculum, instructors, and supportive atmosphere.

Spreading the word that everyone in the organization will require and receive training for appropriate areas and skill levels as part of the TQM implementation allows you to avoid some of the stigma that might otherwise occur from participating in a basic skills training program. The more this position is discussed in meetings, the more it will trickle down to the frontline employees through word of mouth and management attitudes.

Informal Interviews

Informal interview opportunities present themselves often in the workplace and can be purposely sought out to continue the public relations strategy for BSTQ. Use these serendipitous meetings with key personnel as opportunities to gather more data, spread positive perceptions, and to invite others to give input and be part of the program development. These interactions can also be useful as opportunities to listen for "red flag" situations, listen for signs the individual is resisting the process, and to probe for more information regarding concerns the person may have. This constant interaction with all levels of the company allows the program manager to keep a finger on the pulse of the company and implement corrective action before negative perceptions are created.

THE TORO COMPANY

At Toro, the timing for English-as-a-Second-Language (ESL) and BSTQ training was excellent because executives there had perceived the need for this training before the start-up of Philip Crosby's Quality Education System. Toro was just beginning to send managers from the Irrigation Division to the Crosby College. The two levels of personnel, management and frontline workers, were beginning training simultaneously. Positioning basic skills training as one part of an overall company quality initiative and change implementation seemed to be a natural step.

The business goals driving zero-defect performance standards were identified even though there was really no clear picture of the behaviors that were needed to achieve the business goals. The company directors were interviewed individually to clarify executive expectations for the quality initiative. This clarified the requirements for basic skills training.

Management focus groups were held for the purpose of involving all of the management group in the discovery and development part of the basic skills training program. Managers who had not been to the Crosby Quality College were not clear about what additional skills would be needed by the workforce other than speaking English, being accurate with math calculations, and speaking up when they did not understand. Actually, these were the skills that were needed even if there were no changes implemented in the workplace. The program manager had to anticipate that additional skills would be required by the quality initiative.

The supervisors and lead focus groups were not clear on the skills required for the larger goal, but they did know they wanted to be able to communicate in English and have the employees speak up when they did not understand directions.

Involving the frontline workers at Toro in the early discovery process was an important step in disarming the fear level in the workforce. This group volunteered information about how overwhelmed they felt in a class where they could not understand the instructor. They expressed a desire to learn but also a fear of not being able to keep up.

The training was positioned as something for the frontline workers; a curriculum that they could impact by telling us what they wanted to learn. I asked for the group members' help in giving out positive information to the workforce. I followed up this meeting with behaviors that demonstrated that their ideas were being incorporated into the discovery tool and curriculum design.

PIONEER ELECTRONICS TECHNOLOGY, INC. (PET)

The management of PET had identified the goals of becoming certified in ISO 9002, improving communication skills, and increasing the education level of the workforce. English-as-a-Second-Language (ESL) requirements at Pioneer overshadowed any other concerns at the time of the discovery process. Due to the large number of ESL participants at the supervisor/lead levels, the focus groups were mixed, with the determining factor being language fluency. English-speaking managers and other personnel were interviewed individually due to the mixture of levels and locations. Several interviews were conducted at both the Chino facility and the Pomona facility.

In addition to the need for speaking and understanding English, these interviews generated the following data:

What would your like employees to do better?

- Communicate.

- Improve intercompany written and verbal communication.

- Use complete thoughts and sentences.

- Eliminate slow downs, mistakes, and misunderstandings.

- Read process drawings.

- May get wrong tool or part.

- Make sure cuts are accurate.

- Know where to find information and how to access it.

- Read company safety information and regulations.
- Fill out healthcare forms.
- Complete production reports.
- Read directions for model change.
- Complete forms for tracking output, rejects, and rework.
- Ask questions.
- Speak up when they do not understand.

Focus groups consisted of mixed-level groups of employees (workers, supervisors, leads) who primarily spoke Spanish. A few of these employees spoke Asian languages.

The major output of these focus groups was a lengthy vocabulary list which contained nouns (particularly part names and terms for defects) verbs, and adjectives. These words had to do primarily with work instructions and processes. These words were a critical part of the curriculum and their use and understanding were reinforced in many different ways.

SUMMARY OF IMPORTANT POINTS

1. All organizational executives who will evaluate the training should be interviewed in order to identify their expectations and build support for the BSTQ program.

2. Focus groups that are representative of all levels will assist in clarifying expectations of the training.

3. All managers should be included in focus groups.

4. Supervisor focus groups will allow the program manager to identify changes expected by the supervisors as a result of the training.

5. Representatives of frontline workers, including leaders, meeting in focus groups will help spread positive information about the discovery process and BSTQ implementation through the grapevine.

DISCOVER PERCEPTIONS
OF CURRENT SKILL LEVELS

Step 3: Discover Perceptions of Current Skill Levels

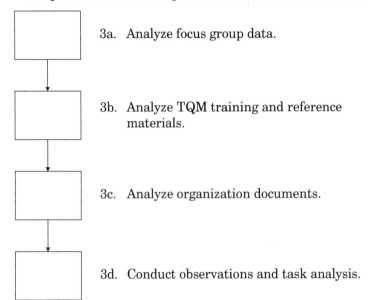

3a. Analyze focus group data.

3b. Analyze TQM training and reference materials.

3c. Analyze organization documents.

3d. Conduct observations and task analysis.

Phase I—Discovery Process

As step 2 of Phase I, Clarify Internal Customer Requirements and Expectations, is completed you can begin to study and analyze the information you have gathered. This next step of the Discovery Phase, Discover Perceptions of Current Skill Levels, consists of the above four parts.

The four activities involved in Discovery Step 3 will be completed by the program manager. He or she will give feedback summaries to the team members who were involved and to other focus group members. This analysis will provide an extensively detailed description of the organization's perception of the major business goals.

The questions suggested in the following list will elicit specific behaviors and detailed descriptions of the organization as it will be when the business goals have been met:

- What will the organization be like when we have reached our goal? (*Is there a clear vision and understanding of what will be happening when the new goals are achieved?*)

- What will we have to learn to do differently to reach our goal? (*Much of the input will refer primarily to what employees need to do now.*)

- What will employees need to do especially well? (*How well do they do this now?*)

- What will we need to do for employees in order to assure the successful achievement of this business goal?

3A. ANALYZE FOCUS GROUP DATA

As the focus group data summary is completed, the skills that do not fit with the others to form a sequential curriculum will be more obvious (see table 3.7.) The summary helps in identifying skills that do not fit with the other skills. Also, characteristics can be identified that will not be focused on specifically but will be improved as a result of BSTQ training.

The first analysis of data from focus groups can be accomplished by performing the following steps:

- Reviewing the data.

- Identifying the most basic skills.

- Identifying the more advanced skills.

- Identifying skills that are too advanced to be included in the instruction schedule.

The program manager will meet with the focus groups again, give them feedback on the data, and ask for further input. This allows the focus group members to identify additional specific skills to include and clarify any of the points that were not clear as the data was organized.

Focus group data can provide information about the existing level of basic workplace skills as perceived by the supervisor, management, and hourly employees, the level of supervisor and management understanding of the changes that will be required by the organization quality initiative, and the existing level of basic supervisory and management skills.

With the focus groups conducted and the data summarized, we can paint a clearer picture of what changes need to take place. In the Toro summary data, (Table 5) the focus group data have been matched with the list of required skills for a total quality management program. You can see that some types of TQM skills are not touched on at all in the focus group data, while several skills for simply getting the job done and being a competent employee are mentioned.

In table 5, some of the basic skills required for total quality are listed in the left column and the Toro focus group data that fits with the total quality skills is positioned in the right column next to the basic skills required for total quality. Some of the total quality categories are not touched in the Toro data. This indicates a lack of familiarity with the total quality program and its targeted results. All of these skills will be critical to total quality success. Some total quality education will be necessary to clarify the desired results of total quality training.

We can look at this comparison and say that the skills required to get the job done have nothing to do with total quality management, so they're not part of the quality training. However, it is a challenge to implement a successful TQM program with a workforce that can not fill out a labor card, follow instructions, or articulate questions. These skills are essential to successful TQM implementation. We can add the following skills to the list of basic workplace skills that must be in place:

Language Skills

- Understanding English (*ESL will increase confidence*).

- Speaking up.

- Understanding and using work-related vocabulary.

- Describing steps in a task.

These language skills are critical to communication that quality improvement requires.

TABLE 5 Toro Summary Data

Skills for Total Quality	Toro Focus Group Data
Learning Skills • Generating and testing hypothesis • Observing and documenting • Unfreezing and reframing— the ability to let go of familiar assumptions and view situations in a different context	• Talk in group • Share information • Be more confident, observant in work area • Understand application and impact • Be more open to changes
Gathering Data • Creating checklists • Writing descriptions • Prioritizing goals • Displaying data (Basic chart construction)	
Problem Solving, Continuous Measurable Improvement • Identifying root cause • Selecting solutions and alternate solutions • Selecting areas of focus • Setting objectives • Action planning • Evaluating results	• Analysis • Read process sheets, specs • More confident, observant in work area

(continued)

Math Skills

• Possessing basic computation skills.

• Understanding basic mathematical processes.

Basic math skills are essential if employees are to assume responsibility for measuring, recording, tracking trends, figuring efficiency, and performing other TQM tasks.

3B. ANALYZE TQM TRAINING AND REFERENCE MATERIALS

Simultaneous with the gathering and summarizing of data from the initial interviews and focus groups, the program manager

TABLE 5 Continued

Skills for Total Quality	Toro Focus Group Data
Communication • Listening • Clarifying meaning, expectation • Confronting conflict —Expressing differences in opinion —Participating in dialogue • Presenting ideas in groups (including presentation skills)	Communication • Organize ideas, composition • Vocabulary to explain and clarify • More involved in meetings and open discussion • Oral communication • Written communication • More English
Working in Teams • Identifying appropriate behavior in team work situation • Validating input of other team members • Planning for timely completion of assignments • Describing problem situations objectively • Brainstorming • Analyzing team process	Presentation Skills • Talk in group • Share information • Express myself better • Recognize other people's level of understanding and be able to communicate with them • Be better team workers • Take initiative • Be more responsible • Be more confident, observant in work area • More involved in meetings and open discussion • Listening, interactions • Ask questions • Work better with other departments • Speak up • Give feedback

should review any materials that are being used for total quality management training and implementation. One purpose of this review is to determine a required reading skill level.

There are many highly reliable readability formulas that might be used. For determining the difficulty level of workplace materials, the FORCAST readability formula is recommended.[1]

---

1. Philippi, Jorie. *Literacy at Work.* New York, NY: Simon & Schuster Workplace Resources, 1991, p. 217.

Originally developed for use with military manuals, FORCAST is designed to compensate for the large number of multisyllabic words commonly contained in workplace technical materials that skew the results of readability formulas used on everyday reading materials. It has a high statistical correlation to other readability formulas and the advantage of being more accurate for use with workplace materials. It is also quick and easy to use.

Furthermore, readability formulas only measure readability, not comprehensibility. Quality training materials present a comprehension challenge for anyone who is not familiar with the concepts or jargon.

Tools for TQM

Some TQM materials are available at different levels of difficulty. For example, Crosby has Quality Awareness, Work Groups, and the Quality Education System (QES) in addition to their Quality College for managers. The text materials for Quality Awareness and Work Groups are formatted with more white space than QES and more diagrams, and each level uses vocabulary and concepts for each level. Training for communication skills and team building are not provided in these materials. Computation of averages and ranges are not taught in Quality Awareness and QES. These are skills that must be learned before the quality improvement processes can be implemented.

Realistically, the organization will choose its quality materials because of the philosophy on which the program is based, not because of its reading level. There is no reason to lower expectations for the organization to meet the educational level of the employees with the least developed basic skills. It is better to raise the skill level of the participants so they can be full partners in the quality efforts of the organization.

The instructor's guide in the TQM materials will be most helpful as you identify activities the TQM training participants will be asked to complete. One way to analyze this material is to review these instructions, listing each instruction given to the participants.

This list of instructions for the participants will probably include things such as:

- List steps in your work process.

- Construct a flowchart of your work process.

- Identify a step in your work process that could be improved.

- Collect the data.

- Determine the type of chart to use.

- Plot the data.

- Figure cost of potential solutions.

- Identify your customers (internal and external).

- Identify customer requirements.

- Work with a problem-solving team.

- Use SPC tools.

- Present your solution to management.

- Assess the effectiveness of your team in managing conflicts.

- Brainstorm ways to improve your team's conflict management skills.

These specific tasks can be analyzed for process steps and basic skills that are required to successfully complete each step. When these basic skills for participating in total quality improvement training are developed in BSTQ, the TQM training can be more effective.

If there are no quality training materials available for analysis, it may be helpful for the curriculum designer to at least understand the guiding principals behind the workplace change that address basic skills. Clarifying the major concepts on which the executive management team is focusing and identifying any phrases or words that will be part of the corporate communications regarding these concepts also will add value to your basic skills training. Concepts and vocabulary that are being used on an organizationwide basis can be defined, clarified, and demystified in a basic skills training program.

These major concepts and vocabulary include the following:

- Total quality policy (usually framed or printed on banners).

- Zero defects.

- Four absolutes (Crosby).

- Quality manual.

- Corrective action documentation.

- HAZMAT (Hazardous Materials) manuals.

3C. ANALYZE ORGANIZATION DOCUMENTS

Written communication and reports can help you ascertain basic skill levels and needed training. Samples may include the following:

- Communication with internal customers.

- Ride share forms.

- Damage reports.

- Job cards.

- Process control charts.

- Efficiency reports.

- Customer complaints.

Try to find the skill requirement commonalities between the different types of forms. These commonalities may include:

- Following directions.

- Using specific vocabulary.

- Using appropriate abbreviations.

- Completing the form correctly.

- Describing nonconformances.

- Counting occurrences.

The identified skill requirement commonalties can generate additional competencies. For example, at Pioneer, one of the greatest needs was clearer, more specific descriptions on damage reports. This need, along with information gathered in focus groups about describing problems, showed that much work was required on workplace vocabulary and basic word order for describing and explaining in English. This included spelling, pronouncing, and using an extensive workplace vocabulary.

Another approach to this paperwork analysis is to record types of errors. On customer complaint records, information regarding basic skill deficiencies may be indicated by the type of complaint. For example, a complaint regarding a wrong shipment of a product may indicate an error in recording model numbers such as reversing digits. This is a common error for people with vision problems. (See question #2 on Math Assessment, Appendix A, for an example of an exercise to diagnose and improve this skill deficiency.)

Conversations with supervisors about their workers' paperwork should occur on an informal basis. One question to ask that will always reveal more information is, "If we could teach the participants one reading, writing, or math skill that would improve the quality of paperwork in your area, what would it be?" This question allows the supervisor to get more specific about a needed skill requirement. Another question could be, "Is there any written task that employees could be doing for you if they had stronger skills?"

If you are the program manager, you can accomplish two things with these questions. You can gather more information about important skill requirements, and you can get the supervisor to identify a benefit to which you can later refer.

Although this information is similar to the information gathered in focus groups, these individual contacts allow the supervisors to identify a skill they may have missed earlier. This also helps to create individual supervisor ownership of the training.

3D. CONDUCT OBSERVATIONS AND TASK ANALYSIS

Another source of information about required skills is the work process itself. The actual work in progress will indicate whether or not the process sheets and flowcharts are followed, and if not, why not. It will show, or the workers will describe, how they get things to work, whether they write it down or not, whether they tell a supervisor and get permission to deviate from a standard, or whether they just do it and don't tell anyone at all. The following are several ways to gather this information, and they can be implemented by either the program manager, a curriculum designer, or an instructor:

- Analyze written job descriptions.

- Analyze written job process sheets.

- Analyze flowcharts of job processes.

- Observe skilled employees performing the job.

- Interview several employees about the steps in the job process.

After completing this analysis of paperwork and observation of frontline employees working, you will have a good understanding of the job processes and the workers' ability to get the information they need in a timely manner. You will also be able to analyze the communication flow and target specific bottlenecks in this flow. With this information you will be able to target the most needed skills for improvement.

Questions and requests that can be helpful in getting critical information from employees include the following:

- Please describe what you do here from the first step to the last step, that is when you hand your work to the next person.

- Which step is the hardest step for you to do?

- Are there any steps that need to be improved? If so, what would you do to improve them? Do you attempt that action? If yes, what happens as a result?

- What would you like to do better?

- What would you like to know more about so you can improve the process?

- What would you like to be able to do better that might effect what you do in the future?

After three or four of these individual or group interviews about job processes, the program manager will begin to define common skill requirements in each of the job processes. These skill requirements may be as basic as describing a problem to a supervisor, or knowing how to check a measurement with a caliper, read a meter, or read a specifications sheet without waiting for a lead person or supervisor to provide the information.

The next step is to identify the skills and abilities that will be required to perform the new work processes and the quality initiative overall, and review the major gaps in skill requirements. One way to do this is to approach the tasks one at a time using the following task analysis worksheets to itemize all possible background skills and knowledge the participants must have.

The task analysis format can be especially useful when interviewing employees about the job. The sample worksheet in Figure 3.1 shows how to use this format when listing steps in a job process.

Summarizing Basic Skill Competency Requirements for Total Quality in Your Company

At this point, data have been gathered from the following:

- Executive interviews.

- Focus groups at all levels.

- Informal interviews with supervisors.

- TQM training materials and ISO certification requirements.

- Paperwork.

- Examples of required paperwork.

- Examples of errors.

- Forms reviewed with supervisors.

- Observations of work in process.

- Interviews with employees about their specific jobs and skill requirements.

1. Identify the steps in doing the task.
2. List the steps of the task in sequential order.
3. For each step in the task, identify the skills and abilities the learner needs to know or perform to be successful at completing the task on the left.

Task: Determine the type of chart to use and how it will be labeled.

Steps in Task	Knowledge, Skills & Abilities
1.0 Select a chart to use.	1.1 Identify the different types of charts.
	1.2 Identify the advantage of each type of chart.
	1.3 Construct each of the different types of charts.
2.0 Decide how to label it.	2.1 Label X and Y axis.
	2.2 Label different charts.
	2.3 Label data for effective presentation.

FIGURE 3.1. **Task Analysis.**

Summarizing and Synthesizing Skill Requirement Data

The process steps for summarizing and synthesizing this information are the following:

1. Using the task analysis worksheet as appropriate, list specific skill requirements for the information from each of the sources of data (interviews, focus groups, training materials, etc.)

2. Transfer the specific skill requirements from each set of information to one sheet of paper.

3. Study all of the lists for common skills.

4. List the common skills on one sheet.

5. Sort and categorize the skills on the list using categories that make sense to your organization (e.g., verbal expression, reading and writing skills, learning and studying skills, and math skills.)

6. Organize skills in each category according to difficulty and their relationship to other skills. Start with the most basic skill (e.g., counting in math, writing the alphabet in reading/writing) and sequence the remaining so that each builds on the previous skill.

7. Get feedback from at least one or two managers. Are these the right skills to focus on for your organization?

THE TORO COMPANY

Focus group data at Toro was gathered on flip charts for the group and on individual worksheets. I then summarized the information for all levels on the computer and printed it as a report to management and the focus groups. In retrospect, it might have seemed valuable to make a distinction in the data summary between data from the frontline employees, the managers, and supervisors. However, summarizing the data together assured anonymity and created the synergy of a total group statement. Actually, the data overlapped between the groups with very little specific to one group only. The result of this Toro data is the list at the end of this case study.

The data from the Toro focus groups could have been valuable as a tool for showing how the training program met customer requirements. Organizing and coding the data would show that the competencies developed later could be cross referenced to the data summary in a more definite way. This can be done for future programs.

The reality of program development is that if the urgency of customer requirements is met, data collection and summarization cannot take forever. At Toro, researching methods of assessment began in June of 1990, assessment began in August, and instruction began in September before the total workforce assessment had been completed. The first groups to be trained were those that were most easily identifiable. Therefore, the best advice here is to avoid getting stuck in *paralysis of analysis.*

If you adhere to traditional approaches to assessment, curriculum development, and training, the flexibility described here is going to be hard to accept. Yet, how can you be responsive to line manager requests for reinforcement of specific skills on a just-in-time basis if the curriculum and the materials are rigidly prescribed? The learning can't be continuously current and applicable to the workplace if the instructional team has all of the materials developed before instruction begins.

The Toro company's corporate headquarters had selected for each of their divisions Philip Crosby's Quality Education System (QES) as the foundation for their quality initiative. The human resources management team at the Irrigation Division in Riverside recognized that these materials would present a challenge to a significant number of their workforce. It was this early recognition that skill deficiencies might keep the division from reaching their goal of implementing cross functional teams that created a need for basic workplace skills training.

During this discovery phase the Crosby materials were analyzed for their reading and comprehension level as well as other needed knowledge and skills that would be required by the workforce to participate in QES and in cross functional teams. The results of this analysis affected the boundaries of BSTQ competencies and curriculum, contributed to a vocabulary list, and added concepts to the curriculum not previously considered.

Tables 6 and 7 represent the data gathered in the discovery focus groups at The Toro Company. Some of the data could easily be sorted into general categories of writing, math, and communication on the first cut. This first step in summarizing the data is shown to you to illustrate how simple this analysis can be. The same questions were asked of manager, supervisor, and frontline worker focus groups, except for, "What would you like your employees to do better?" This question was replaced with "What would you like other employees to do better?" The responses to these questions have been quoted just as they were written, so their meaning is not absolutely clear. The second focus groups provide an opportunity to clarify answers and ask for additional ideas.

The focus group data can be condensed into a general description of a curriculum for basic works skills. The topics listed

TABLE 6 Summary of Data from Toro Focus Groups

What would you like your employees to do better?

Writing
- Reports
- Forms
- Penmanship
- Grammar
- Filling out job card
- Organize ideas, composition
- Analysis

Math Computation
- Accuracy in computation
- Eliminate simple mistakes
- Accurate counts
- Record data
- Addition
- Subtraction
- Long Division
- Percentages
- Averages
- Conversions
- Measurements
- Algebra
- Use calculator

Communication
- Meetings
- More involved in meetings and open discussion
- Giving feedback
- Speak up
- Phone with customer
- Understand English, especially instructions
- Listening, interactions
- Ask questions (Quality Awareness)
- Work better with other departments
- Vocabulary to explain and clarify
- Fill out labor cards using written commands and numbers

(continued)

61

TABLE 6 Continued

What would you like your employees to do better?

Read process sheets

Use a computer

Depend on one's self, make decisions
  • Take initiative
  • Be more responsible (care more)
  • More confident/observant in work area

Follow through

Follow instructions

Understand the importance of attendance

Be better teamworkers

Understand application and impact

Planning
  • Scheduling
  • Focusing on goals
  • Managing time

More open to changes

TABLE 7 Summary of Data from Toro Focus Groups

What would you like to do better?

Nonexempt Employee Focus Group

Oral Communication

Written Communication
  • Spelling
  • Organization
  • Reading, writing, vocabulary
  • Reading specs
  • Writing skills and reports
  • Handwriting

More English

Computation

Presentation skills (public speaking)
  • Talk in group
  • Share information
  • Express myself better

(continued)

TABLE 7 Continued

What would you like to do better?

Supervisor/Manager Focus Groups
  Gain confidence of employees
  Assertiveness (feedback)
  Conducting meetings
  Participate
  Train people better
  Instruct
  Facilitate
  Delegate
  Reviews and evaluations
  • giving them
  • writing them
  Recognize other people's level of understanding and be able to communicate with them
  Meet deadlines, time management
  Learn computer
  Understand technical manuals
  Technical knowledge
  • Electronics, robotics
  Procedures on scrap
  Receiving procedures
  Know parts
  Cross trained; understand all jobs
  Understand quality procedures and technology
  Correct attitudes
  Problem identification (depth perception)
  • resourcefulness
  Facilitation
  Influencing/Selling
  Management skills
  Organize, prioritize, delegate
  Quote jobs better
  Implement more changes
  More attention to detail work

(continued)

TABLE 7 Continued

What would you like your manager to do better?

Understand and communicate with people where they are (at employee level)

Give information

(When we don't get it we feel unimportant, not good enough.)

More communication
 • Listen
 • Believe we know
 • Value us give us more information

More understanding of our job and what we need
 • Physically do the job

Better leadership skills
 • Feedback, constructive criticism

Listen

Now they say you're important, don't show it. Let them show it.

Communicate one to one

Receptive attitude

Dealing with conflict
 • Problem solving
 • Valuing differences, different ideas, styles
 • Basic conversation too high above us. Ask questions.

Motivation
 • Remove fear, let them know why
 • Give long range goals for personal development

Communicating task information

Empowering employees

Trust

Credibility

in Table 8 will need to be introduced in ESL classes for those employees who need ESL instruction.

The focus group data can be further condensed and organized in the next cut at summarizing, as shown in Table 9. In this summary, the curriculum topics become more evident. Table 10 describes improvements possible through BSTQ and Table 11 lists participants' responses to focus group data that may indicate a lack of job skills.

TABLE 8 Summarized Toro Data for Basic Skills Curriculum Development and ESL Curriculum (Prerequisite to BSTQ)

ESL: English

Understand English, especially follow instructions.

Instructions   Work vocabulary

Oral communication

Speak up (*ESL will increase confidence and clarify business culture*)

Talk in group

Express myself better

Ask questions

Counting, numbers

TABLE 9 Curriculum Topics

Reading and Writing BSTQ Curriculum	
Work vocabulary	Understand English, especially instructions
Follow instructions	
Forms	Ask questions
Reports	Vocabulary to explain and clarify
Handwriting	Fill out labor cards using written commands and numbers
Spelling	
Grammar	Read Process sheets
Fill out job card	Talk in group
Organize ideas, composition	Express myself better
	Speak up

Math BSTQ Curriculum	
Math Computation	
—Accuracy in computation	—Long division
—Eliminate simple mistakes	—Percentages
—Accurate counts	—Averages
—Record data	—Conversions
—Addition	—Measurements
—Subtraction	

TABLE 10 BSTQ Improvements

Possible Improvement as Result of BSTQ, Not Specific Curriculum

Depend on self, make decisions
  Be more responsible (care more)
  More confident/observant in work area

Be better team workers
  More involved in meetings and open discussion
  Give feedback

Communicate on the phone with customer
  Analysis

Not Included in Toro Basic Skills Curriculum

Algebra
Calculator skills

TABLE 11 Areas for Improvement

Focus Group Data Responses That Indicate Lack of Ordinary Job Skills

Writing
  Reports, forms, job cards
  Fill out labor cards using written commands and numbers

Follow instructions

Understand the importance of attendance

Manage time

Know parts

Cross trained, understand all jobs

Correct attitudes

Computation

Communicating task information

English
  • Understand English, especially instructions
  • Scheduling

PIONEER ELECTRONICS TECHNOLOGY, INC. (PET)

At Pioneer Electronics Technology, most of the managers were interviewed personally or in small groups. As indicated earlier, the major issue at PET was English-as-a-Second-Language (ESL) requirements. Focus groups mostly centered around English skills, even at the supervisor level where the primary language in one facility was Spanish. The major result of the focus groups at Pioneer was the production of a large English vocabulary list for the ESL curriculum which was also used for the reading and writing part of the BSTQ curriculum. These vocabulary words were used to describe job process steps, write descriptions of damage, clarify directions, and many other production-related exercises. The focus groups indicated a critical need for reading, writing, and understanding work-related vocabulary, and there were many requirements that could not even be identified until the language issues were addressed.

Pioneer had not elected to do training in quality management or processes at this time but focused on clarifying processes and achieving ISO 9002 certification. Therefore, there were no materials to analyze except for the vocabulary that was identified in the focus groups, the process charts in one location, and the job process steps at both locations. Toward the end of the program the instructors worked with the learners on the ISO 9002 audit questions that needed clarifying and answering.

Some of the basic tasks required for ISO 9002 certification are the following:

Documentation

- Describing specific steps and behaviors in detail.

- Sequencing specific process steps.

- Using clear language versus technical or academic terms.

- Reading and interpreting process charts, drawings, and schematics.

Communication

- Eliciting information and clarification from others (questioning, clarifying).

- Listening.

- Clarifying meaning and expectations.

- Confronting conflict.

- Expressing differences in opinion.

- Participating in dialogue.

- Presenting ideas in groups (including presentation skills).

Working in Teams

- Using appropriate behavior in teamwork situations.

- Validating input of other team members.

- Planning for timely completion of assignments.

- Describing problem situations objectively.

- Brainstorming.

- Analyzing team processes.

Pioneer had translated each article in their newsletter into Spanish in an attempt to communicate with the Hispanic workforce. While this effort is commendable, it was not the answer to total communication because many of the frontline workers had limited literacy skills in their own language. There also were other languages represented. One of the goals at Pioneer was to eliminate in the near future the Spanish translation of this newsletter and other employee communication. At that time all employee communication would be written in English.

SUMMARY OF IMPORTANT POINTS

- Focus group information allows you to identify some of the changes these representative groups will expect as a result of the training.

- Focus group data give you a general idea of the skills that are lacking in the target population.

- Analysis of TQM materials is a way to identify tasks the workforce will be expected to perform when TQM is in place.

- Analysis of workplace documents will identify common nonconformances.

- Employees who lack the basic skills to participate in the TQM effort will not be as involved as they could be if they were prepared.

ASSESS BASIC SKILLS OF THE WORKFORCE

Step 4: Assess the Basic Skills of the Workforce

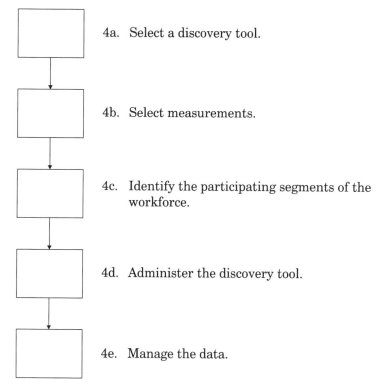

4a. Select a discovery tool.

4b. Select measurements.

4c. Identify the participating segments of the workforce.

4d. Administer the discovery tool.

4e. Manage the data.

Phase I—Discovery Process

This step consists of the above five interconnected parts.

Assessing basic skill levels helps identify the current basic skill levels of the workforce. This step will be a reality check and confirmation for the organization regarding existing skill levels, and an introduction of the impending changes in skills required by the organization's business goals of quality improvement, reengineering, or ISO 9000 certification.

The assessment data are useful for several purposes including the following:

- Grouping participants.
- Indicating common strengths and deficiencies.
- Providing baseline data which can be used in post assessment.
- Reframing perceptions of the workforce skill level (Toro thought they had an extensive lack of English language skill among the frontline workers. The assessment discovered only 67 ESL participants out of over 500 employees. It was actually discovered that the major ESL issue existed within the temporary workforce.)
- Identifying employees who may have ESL needs but also have high math skills.

4A. SELECT A DISCOVERY TOOL

An action step that can be taken simultaneously with conducting focus groups is the review of the instruments available for assessing workforce skill levels. The selection of this instrument will effect the success of the entire program and should be made with this consideration. A basic-skills assessment can create a highly volatile employee relations issue if not addressed carefully. Assessment of the native-English-speaking workforce is more precarious than the assessment of the ESL workforce. For the native speakers, this assessment is a threat (perceived or real) of exposing their school failures and inadequacies. Every precaution should be taken to alleviate these fears in order to have a successful training program.

Assessment requires close involvement of the program manager from instrument selection through administration and data management. It is the responsibility of the program manager to investigate assessment tools and present a recommendation to the program management team.

It is helpful to determine the goal for the assessment. Is the goal to identify levels of basic workforce skills so the organization can provide training for successful participation in the quality improvement environment? Or is the goal to assess academic achievement and gather statistical data?

I strongly recommend that an assessment be selected or created with the intent of finding out what the BSTQ training must do for the employees so they will be empowered to function competently in the total quality, high-performance environment. Keeping the focus on organizational goals and workplace requirements will reassure participants that they will not be subjected to the stigma of grade-level placement or pass-fail judgments.

I suggest using a customized assessment or discovery instrument over a standardized assessment. But the individual organization needs to weigh the pros and cons associated with each. Some of the characteristics of each type of assessment are compared in Table 12.

4B. SELECT MEASUREMENTS

Once the program manager and department managers have determined what the assessment should measure, the type of assessment tool can be selected. If statistically valid measurements that indicate grade levels are the goal, use a standardized assessment. Don't waste time creating one.

TABLE 12 Customized versus Standardized Assessment

Customized	Standardized
Nonthreatening, can resemble material from work. May remind participant of past testing experience.	Appears official, will probably remind participant of past testing experience.
Assesses levels of competency achievement. Does not assess grade levels.	Reports an official ranking (e.g., grade level).
Based on work competency achievement.	Grade levels are tied to childhood norms.
Not statistically valid unless company spends large quantity of time and money on validation.	Statistically valid (although sometimes legally questioned).
Assesses skills on work-related material.	Assesses skills on unrelated vocabulary and computations.
Administration to large numbers is labor intensive.	Easily administered to large numbers.

If a customized assessment is selected, it can be constructed to measure the most important skills for the business goals. It can also be constructed to resemble written materials found in the specific workplace.

Using the focus group data, select the most basic skills in each major category such as math, reading and writing, study skills, on other appropriate grouping for the data with which you are working.

Then, decide how much time the assessment should take. I recommend creating one 30-minute assessment for reading, writing, and study skills and one 30-minute assessment for math and graphs.

Next, pilot the assessment with groups similar to the target population to make sure it can be completed in that amount of time.

Figure scores at 70, 80, and 90 percent of the total possible score and determine the level of scores that will indicate a need for BSTQ training.

Because this is an assessment of very basic skills, even an 80 percent achievement level score may not be high enough to preclude participation in training. My experience is that 85 to 90 percent is an effective cut off point. By the time the company has trained all of the employees that scored below 85 percent, the others will have gotten the message that basic skills are important. That awareness alone may increase the functioning skill level of the workforce.

4C. IDENTIFY THE PARTICIPATING SEGMENTS OF THE WORKFORCE

A key element in the development of a successful program is identifying the population to be assessed for the existing level of basic skills. Although assessing everyone's basic skills, including managers, might appear to show equality, doing so would not respect the intelligence of the employees who know that not everyone is a candidate for basic skills training. They will assume that the directors and probably the middle managers do not need basic reading, writing, or computation skills training.

The program management team (possibly with input from the organization's legal advisor) must establish criteria for employee participation in this skill discovery process. The criteria may be different for each organization; they might consist of formal education levels, employee grade levels, functional assignments, or whatever seems to be a natural cut-off point for the organization.

The program manager will need to be alert to feelings of uncertainty and conflict as to why the discovery process is being conducted and why it includes some people and not others. Each potential conflict is an opportunity to position the discovery process as a way to find out what training the organization needs to provide for each employee level. A response to anyone with concerns about who is being assessed could be, "Presently, the focus is on *job levels 2 and 3* and this is how we are assessing those needs. Other levels will be assessed in different ways."

English as a Second Language (ESL)

The English-as-a-Second-Language (ESL) component was an important element of both case study programs. California has a large minority workforce, many of whom are first generation immigrants. Others continue to live with families where the native language is spoken at home. Often, the children who are in school serve as translators and connecting links to the English-speaking world. The tendency to group together in neighborhoods where their customs and language are maintained decreases their necessity to learn English.

Assessing English-as-a-Second-Language Skills

Some employees may need English-as-a-Second-Language training before they can participate in BSTQ classes. An ESL assessment is separate from the BSTQ assessment and should be addressed by instructors who are experienced with this population. Always involve the organization's own legal council in reviewing the assessment plan as legal guidelines differ from one area to another in content and in interpretation. The instructors can assess the verbal language skill level of each individual, recommend a level of ESL instruction for each, and provide vocational ESL instruction that will prepare this group for BSTQ participation. There are external consulting companies that provide this service. Another possible source is community adult basic education services that use more traditional methods. There are pluses and minuses to each and these will vary by locality.

An adequate ESL assessment can be conducted by qualified instructors using the oral Basic English Skills Test (BEST) Language Assessment, a standardized assessment which measures levels of language fluency instead of grade levels (BEST materials can be obtained through the ALTA Book Center). Since this assessment is oral, it does not create the same apprehension levels that a standardized written assessment creates. The assessor can manage the impact of this assessment through their own nonverbal behavior and manner of verbal delivery. This ESL assessment is less time consuming than the written BSTQ assessment and quickly identifies levels of ESL skills which can be used to form classes in ESL as a prerequisite for BSTQ training.

Because this ESL assessment is an integral part of the total program, its progress should be closely monitored by the program manager. However, I have not experienced the degree of resistance with ESL participants that I have with other employees being assessed for BSTQ skills. For the most part, employees who need ESL instruction are very pleased to be getting it and are grateful to the organization for providing it. Although many levels of ability exist in the ESL group, it tends to be a very motivated group of learners.

Within this group of employees who qualify for ESL training, there will be several different levels of ability and fluency. For our purposes I will describe them in the following two definite groups:

- Nonnative English speakers who have little fluency.

- Very fluent nonnative English speakers.

Within the group that is not fluent, there can be several levels of fluency, the lowest being preliterate in both languages. This means they have no decoding skills in either their native language or English.

The profiles of these subgroups in the population to be assessed are described as follows.

Nonnative English speakers. The nonnative English speakers, or ESL participants as they will be referred to, are the most visible group and are therefore quite easily identified for BSTQ assessment. They usually speak very little English and speak their native language with other employees. These employees first should be assessed for English language understanding and speaking ability. Usually, if the assessment is announced, employees who need to take it will volunteer. They will also inform each other that an ESL assessment is taking place in order to place employees in ESL training. If the assessment indicates a need for ESL training, that should be provided before they enter a BSTQ program.

Fluent nonnative English speakers. Some nonnative English speakers become quite adept with verbal English but lack the education background that develops strong written language skills. Additionally, their English-speaking ability often camouflages their lack of understanding. This group of fluent nonnative English speakers presents some interesting training challenges, which will be explained as we discuss the training population more specifically. This group must also have ESL classes before being assessed for BSTQ, but they will probably need only one 40- to 48-hour session of ESL.

Assessing BSTQ skills of native English speakers

The most resistance to assessment and instruction may be found in the group of native speakers of English. The employees in this category who qualify for the BSTQ assessment have often had at least one unpleasant experience in their years of education. If that is the case, visions of crowded classes, humiliation, lack of success, failure, and even ridicule are easily created for them by the sight of a classroom. The suggestion that employees in this group may lack basic skills attacks their ego at the most personal levels. If these employees have worked for the company for several years, they have successfully performed their jobs without using these skills. This allows the program management and instruction teams to emphasize that everyone forgets what they don't use on a regular basis and the purpose of the assessment is to find out what they need to learn. When a learner in this group resists attending the assessment, it is best to validate their right to resist.

The key is to not force participation, but let the participant decide to participate or not. Eventually, as the program creates a history of success, they may ask to be involved.

Native English-speaking supervisors. In the traditional organizational environment of the past, an employee who was good at his or her job, especially at being able to increase production, got along reasonably well with the other employees to the point of being an informal leader and stayed around long enough to be promoted first to lead and then to supervisor. He or she was not trained for the new position of authority and often accomplished the job by working harder and longer than before.

In some cases, this method of career development allowed employees to advance to a fairly high level without their lack of basic skills being discovered. In the traditional organization, these skills were not as visible as they are in today's quality-oriented, high-performance organization. Employees at this level who face participating in quality training sessions with their peers and later with cross functional teams may fearfully face an insecure future. These special situations should be handled discretely, with sensitivity and compassion, by the program manager and other appropriate personnel.

4D. ADMINISTER THE DISCOVERY TOOL

Once the discovery tool is designed, the program manager can test it with individuals who have different levels of skills. In the case of the first discovery tool that was designed for BSTQ, it was tested and timed with several different age groups including bright elementary school students, well-educated English-as-a-Second-Language foreign exchange students and educated adults outside of manufacturing. This testing provided a feel for the feasibility of finishing each of the assessments (language and math) in a 30-minute time period. It also showed where the discovery tool needed to be made clearer. This was also an effective method of proofreading.

The program manager then piloted the assessment with a group of assembly employees. They gave input on areas that were difficult to understand and recommended changes to the format. This was the only assessment they were asked to take.

These employees were selected by the program management team because of their informal leadership roles and the public relations benefits of having them included in the instrument development and approval process. This was part of the positioning strategy for the discovery process and the training to follow.

I am reminded of a suggestion for successful change; "Light many little fires." All of the groups which gave input in the beginning were part of a successful attempt to "light many little fires," creating interest and support for the program at several levels.

With the focus groups completed, the data summarized for the groups, and the discovery tools developed and piloted, the assessment part of the discovery phase can begin.

The assessment can be successfully conducted in groups of 20 to 30 people. Assessment groups larger than 30 people tend to be impersonal and intimidating for the participants.

The person who introduces and administers this assessment can be the program manager or one of the instructors familiar with the discovery process. This person should be someone who has some connection with BSTQ program management. This will enhance the program as a positive opportunity for the employees and to build trust for the instruction team.

As an introduction to the assessment, the administrator will need to:

- Warmly welcome the participants.

- Introduce the BSTQ training as a positive opportunity for employees who are valued by the organization.

- Introduce the assessment as a way to tell the program instructors what the learners need to know.

- Assure the participants that assessment scores will not be provided to Personnel or their managers or anyone else at all.

4E. MANAGE THE DATA

The issue of having adequate basic skills attacks the human ego at a very deep, personal level. Not having engineering skills does not label a person as inadequate. Not having team membership skills usually implies inexperience rather than inadequacy, but not having basic skills indicates that a person does not measure up to basic expectations in a literate society. The fragile human self-concept must be nurtured and strengthened if this type of training is to be successful. Therefore, every aspect of gathering and managing the discovery data is important.

Even though the customized assessment may require hand scoring, that data can be entered into a computer database which can be used for many training-related purposes. This tracking system should be in place when the assessment begins and should be maintained by the program manager, separate from all other personnel records.

Managing this data is an opportunity to build trust for the entire program by honoring the organization's commitment to confidentiality. Employees are concerned about how the scores will be used and who will know about them. Supervisors have been known to request this data for employee assignment purposes or as evidence of an employee's capability. BSTQ scores must not be used for the purpose of employment decisions regarding full-time personnel.

THE TORO COMPANY

When an assessment instrument was being chosen for Toro, several standardized tests were reviewed including the Comprehensive Adult Student Assessment System (CASAS) and the Test of Adult Basic Education (TABE.) At the same time, an actual case study was brought to my attention that involved a large company with a division in another state. This company chose a local community college adult education department to assess their workforce. They implemented the assessment using the TABE and of a group of 160 employees, 90 of them got up and walked out before the assessment could be completed. It was these considerations that brought about a bias for customized assessments at Toro Irrigation and at Pioneer Electronics Technology, Inc.

Once the goal of the discovery tool, to identify training to increase the ability of current employees to function in total quality training and in the future TQM environment, and the criteria for creating the tool were clear, the design was not as difficult as it had originally seemed.

Toro Irrigation's criteria for an effective discovery tool was the following:

- It would not resemble a standardized test and therefore would not be answered on a computer-scored answer sheet.

- Performance would not be timed.

- Content would be based on workplace communication and requirements.

- Discovery tool exercises would represent several levels of achievement.

- Correct grammar and punctuation would not be assessed except as it effected understanding.

With this criteria identified, the design of the Toro Irrigation discovery tool could proceed. After reviewing existing assessments and Toro's goal and criteria for a discovery tool, the discovery assessment that was used for the Toro assessment was developed. Considering the Toro focus group data, the areas to be assessed were determined to be the following (see sample assessment in Appendix A):

Reading/Writing Concepts

1. Write the English alphabet.

2. Read simple sentence beginnings and complete the sentence.

3. Select the correct meaning of a common work-action word.

4. Match work-related abbreviations to the correct words.

5. Sequence the steps in a common process.

6. Read an actual communication example from a memo or manual and select the correct answer to a comprehension question.

7. Comprehend the information on a common company form.

8. Demonstrate a comprehension of charts by selecting appropriate information.

9. List examples of a characteristic.

10. Describe the steps in an individual job process and list them in sequence.

11. Follow simple written directions.

Math Assessment Concepts

1. Count the number of objects accurately.

2. Recognize numbers, identify differences in multiple digit numbers.

3. Tabulate hatch marks.

4. Addition (two, three, and four columns, no renaming; two, three, and four columns, with renaming).

5. Subtraction (two and three columns, no renaming, two and three columns, with renaming).

6. Multiplication (one and two digit multipliers with no renaming; one and two digit multipliers with renaming).

7. Division (recognizing division signs, simple division, one digit quotient with remainder, and two digit quotient [long division]).

8. Fractions (changing improper fractions to mixed numbers).

9. Order decimals.

10. Hours and minutes.

11. Write percentages as decimals.

12. Write decimals as percentages.

13. Use line graphs.

14. Interpret control charts.

15. Record sample measurements.

16. Figure averages.

17. Figure ranges.

The first group at Toro to be assessed in BSTQ was the advanced ESL group. This group tested too high for ESL instruction on verbal fluency levels. The BSTQ assessment gave us reading- and math-skill information in addition to what we knew about their language abilities. From that group, we continued assessing employees in small groups that were selected with regard for production schedules. One technique that worked well for this scheduling included to the following:

1. Ask the supervisor how many employees he or she could spare off the production line at any given time.

2. Schedule the assessment times and indicate that each supervisor is to send the pre-identified number of employees to each assessment.

3. Ask the employees to sign in when they attend their assessment session.

This method of filtering employees into the assessment is much simpler for both the supervisors and the assessors when there is a large number to assess. The final count for assessment at Toro was over 550 employees. At Pioneer Electronics there were half that many and they were divided between two plants, so individuals could be assigned to sessions more easily. At first, Toro wanted to have everyone in the company go through the basic skills assessment. This approach, while showing good intentions, would have been wasteful in regards to both time and material. If assessing everyone was not wise, then what criteria would be used for selecting the employee group for assessment? The human resources team, which consisted of the director, a manager, and myself, decided that the assessment population would include everyone with less than an associate's degree from a junior college in the United States. Other employees would be assessed at the appropriate skill level for their positions (e.g., managers and engineers would be assessed in different ways). Again, the management team and the general manager reemphasized the position that everyone would be going through training and the organization was in the process of determining appropriate training for all employees.

Therefore, the population to be assessed for basic skill proficiency at Toro was determined to include only job-level-3 employees. Within this population there existed the following four distinct groups:

- Nonnative English speakers.

- Verbally fluent nonnative English speakers.

- Native English speakers.

- Supervisors and leads.

The first group to be assessed were the nonnative English speakers. Candidates for this group were referred by supervisors who had to make judgments regarding language ability. A few of these employees were referred because their supervisors had observed that they spoke a language on the line other than English.

One of the women who had been referred for an assessment based on this criteria became very angry during the ESL assessment and walked out. As program manager, I was informed immediately and I asked her to come back and talk with me. As we talked, I first gave her permission to refuse the assessment, then I inquired into her strong resentment at having been sent. I checked her perception of the reason she was referred for assessment and of what being in the training could mean to her.

She described her suspicions that she had been sent because her name was of Hispanic origin and because the supervisor wanted to prove she was not doing her job. This gave me an opportunity to learn more about her, where she came from, and how she felt about work. She described being educated in the United States and speaking Spanish at home. She shared information about her family and the fact that although she spoke English fluently, she was not comfortable writing it, and she could use a brush up on math.

I presented the benefits of the language and math training, empathized with her regarding not understanding why she had been sent, and asked her if she would like to skip the assessment and still come to the first class for fluent nonnative English speakers. She accepted and now, five years later, she calls to me on the manufacturing floor to say hello. Her experience in the class was positive for all of us.

The ESL language training needs at Toro were much less than had been estimated in the beginning, but the math deficiencies were much greater than had been anticipated. With this information from the discovery process, the focus of the curriculum shifted from ESL needs to basic skill deficiencies in the total employee population, primarily in math. This proficiency in basic math is important in improving accuracy of counts and calculations, understanding SPC, and understanding and using formulas for figuring efficiency and earned hour ratio as examples.

At Toro, there were two valued supervisors who had shown deficiencies in basic skills. At the first sign of their discomfort in focus groups, I took them aside and talked to them about their avoidance of written work. They volunteered the information that they could neither read nor write. The supervisors were exempted from the written assessment, interviewed personally, and referred to the local adult education lab where they began working with interactive computer programs in basic reading skills. These programs held their interest and they attended regularly. As program manager, I had frequent personal contact with them for several months and observed that they were doing some work on their own. Both individuals expressed relief that they no longer had to hide their skill deficiencies and were now doing something about it. They were supported in their efforts by the instructors in the quality classes.

Other supervisors at Toro were assessed in peer groups. Their assessment was customized for them and was slightly more difficult than the assessment used for the assembly employees.

At Toro, it was determined that no assessment scores would be given out in order to reduce the tendency to compare individual ability. It was announced, however, that employees who really wanted to know their individual scores could make an appointment with the program manager and review them in private. The opportunity to review scores in private was extended to those supervisors, office staff, and other employees who completed the assessment.

Scores for the supervisor assessments, along with feedback on development requirements, were addressed in meetings between individual participants and the program manager. Classes for this group were not scheduled at this time. This presented an opportunity to make these employees aware of areas for improvement and so that they could begin to work to improve, either on their own or in a local class.

TABLE 13 Toro Assessment Data

Assessment for Factory	Total	Percent of Total
Employee Assessments	539	100%
Total Scoring Below 80%	237	44%
Total Scoring Below 70%	116	22%
Scoring Below 70%, English Only	16	39%
Scoring Below 70%, Math Only	60	11%
Scoring Below 70%, English and Math	40	7%

Table 13 provides an overview of the assessment data at Toro.

PIONEER ELECTRONICS TECHNOLOGY, INC. (PET)

The Pioneer discovery tool was similar to the Toro model, but was customized using exercises based on PET literature, documents, and math requirements.

Pioneer used the same criteria that the program manager and human resources managers used at Toro to select candidates for the BSTQ program. However, most of the employees were part of the nonnative-English-speaking group, including a group of supervisors and leads. Because there was great understanding of the ESL population, and because this organization consisted of two small facilities where the employees were well known individually, the ESL candidates were easily identified.

Due to the language requirements of the English-as-a-Second-Language program, the supervisors who were all ESL learners took the same written assessment as other factory employees.

The demographic groups that were included in the assessment at Pioneer were:

- Nonnative English speakers.

- Verbally fluent nonnative English speakers.

- Native English speakers.
- Nonnative-English-speaking supervisors and leads.

The original assessment data for PET is presented in Table 14 and 15.

SUMMARY OF IMPORTANT POINTS

- Determine definite criteria for including employees in the BSTQ assessment.
- Different demographic groups with some different and some similar needs may require BSTQ training.
- Do not use grade school norms for scoring assessments.

TABLE 14 PET Assessment Data, Chino Facility

Assessments for Chino Facility	Total	Percent of Total
Total Nonexempt Assessed	134	100%
Native English Speakers (NS)	22	16%
NS Scoring Below 80% Reading/Writing	6	4%
NS Scoring Below 80% Math	16	7%
NS Scoring Below 80% Both	6	4%
English as Second Language (ESL)	112	84%
ESL Scoring Below 80% Reading/Writing	90	67%
ESL Scoring Below 80% Math	109	81%
ESL Scoring Below 80% Both	89	66%
ESL Scoring Below 70% Both	74	55%
ESL Scoring Below 50% Both	40	30%

TABLE 15 PET Assessment Data, Pomona Facility

Assessments for Pomona Facility	Total	Percent of Total
Total Nonexempt	134	100%
Total Nonexempt Assessed	77	57%
Nonnative Speakers (ESL) Not Assessed (Written)	57	43%
NS & ESL Scoring Below 80% Both	67	87%
NS & ESL Scoring Below 50% Reading/Writing	44	57%
NS & ESL Scoring Below 50% Math	25	32%
NS & ESL Scoring Below 50% Both	37	48%

- ESL learners need conversational, vocational English classes before entering BSTQ.

- Do not post assessment scores. Keep scores confidential.

- An assessment should be used as a guide for placing learners in situations where they will get the support they need to be successful on the job.

DEVELOPMENT

SELECT AND DEVELOP AN INSTRUCTION TEAM

Step 1: Select and Develop an Instruction Team

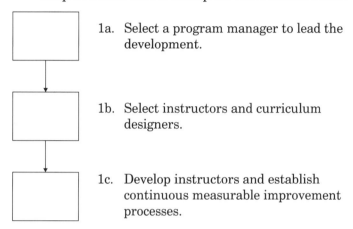

1a. Select a program manager to lead the development.

1b. Select instructors and curriculum designers.

1c. Develop instructors and establish continuous measurable improvement processes.

Phase II—Development Process

The development phase of a BSTQ program that is work-related and customized for the individual organization consists of the following three steps:

1. Select and develop an instruction team.

2. Identify the curriculum and competencies.

3. Develop the curriculum and materials.

Step 1 of the Development Phase, Select and Develop an Instruction Team, consists of the following three interconnected parts:

1a. Select a program manager to lead the development.

1b. Select instructors and curriculum designers.

1c. Develop instructors and establish continuous measurable improvement processes.

The second phase of the BSTQ program, Development, begins before the first phase is completed. Activities of each of the phases may take place in concert with one another. The boundaries between the steps in each of the phases; Discovery, Development, and Implementation, and even between the phases themselves, can sometimes blur. There is no need to complete each phase before going on to the next. This would take away one of the benefits of such a program—the ability to change, grow, and learn constantly from the process.

In fact, both the discovery phase and the development phase should be ongoing throughout the completion of the implementation phase. This occurs daily through constant communication with internal customers in the classroom and throughout the organization. Constant communication allows the internal customers to have input into the curriculum and ownership for the success of the training. This will allow the program to change and grow on a daily basis. In this way it will be always open to better methods, more relevant material, better processes, and continuous improvement. The individual steps are presented separately but in reality, this program should be organic and flexible, with structure added by the objectives, competencies, and schedule. The following Plan, Do, Check, Act cycle can be used at several levels from the beginning to the end of this program implementation.

PDCA	BSTQ Program
Plan	Discovery phase. Development phase.
Do	Implementation phase.
Check	Feedback to/from focus groups. Feedback on beginning sessions. Constant feedback from internal customers. Evaluation.
Act	Make additions or corrections to curriculum.

The selection of an instruction team can and should begin simultaneously with the beginning of the skills assessment. As with any hiring process, finding instructors may take longer than intended, so it is best to begin immediately. The instruction team members include the program manager, who serves on both the program management team and the instruction team, the program designers, and the instructors.

1A. SELECT A PROGRAM MANAGER TO LEAD THE DEVELOPMENT

As soon as the company executives decide to begin the BSTQ process, a program manager should be selected, as discussed in chapter 1. In addition to the required skills also discussed earlier, the program manager will be responsible for selecting and developing the instruction team and assuring program quality. The program manager can accomplish this by supporting the instructors with positive and constructive feedback.

1B. SELECT INSTRUCTORS AND CURRICULUM DESIGNERS

I have no statistically valid data to indicate that instructors who have primarily academic experience find it difficult to understand the pressures of business. However, my experience in academia leads me to conclude that this is true. In the academic setting the focus is the classroom and the teaching/learning exchange that goes on there. The entire academic organization,—university, community adult school, or other public institution—supports that focus.

In the business setting, the classroom is seen not only as subsidiary to business goals but it is sometimes perceived as a barrier to meeting those goals. The program manager and instructors must be sensitive to the critical pressures of business and adopt an attitude that allows them to partner with management, staff, and operations for successful implementation. At the same time, the integrity and focus of the training program must be assertively maintained or the organization will be unhappy with the training later on.

As in any employee selection process, there are some qualifications that the candidate must have to be successful and there are some qualifications that would be nice to find in a candidate but which can be developed. These qualifications are listed in Table 16.

TABLE 16 Characteristics that instructor must have at selection time

- Is able to explain concepts simply.
- Is able to create and use practical examples.
- Demonstrates respect for and understanding of an adult basic skill learner.
- Is nondefensive and can accept criticism.
- Is a good listener and speaker.
- Has a positive problem-solving attitude.
- Is flexible and adjusts to change.
- Is able to work as a team player.

Characteristics that can be developed include the following:

- Has the ability to identify learning competency requirements in workplace materials.
- Understands the nonacademic environment.
- Has concern for company business and training goals.

Because the criteria in this checklist tend to be subjectively determined, it helps to use a worksheet similar to the following Resource Worksheet when interviewing instructor candidates. The comments and questions in italics underneath each statement are offered as a guide to creating your own questions. This worksheet is an effective method of gathering data during an interview and its basis is the idea that past behavior is a good indicator of future performance.

Determining Instructor Fees

It is difficult in the beginning stages of a program to know how to structure subcontracted instructor fees. If you have been subcontracting with business trainers, you know that the number of hours of training required to develop strong basic work skills would be very expensive using business trainer fee schedules. The following is a guideline that I have found has worked well.

My research into instructor fees identified the highest level of instructor pay in the local adult basic education programs. I then theorized if I calculated a low-end prep time such as 25 to 33 percent of classroom time for which they would be paid, the

INSTRUCTOR SELECTION WORKSHEET

Candidate Name_____   Date_____

In each of the following behavioral descriptions, rate the candidate on a scale of 0 (Behavior Not Exhibited) to 5 (Behavior Exhibited Consistently). Record specific observations where possible.

Characteristic   **Extent Behavior is Exhibited**

1. Is able to explain concepts simply.   0 1 2 3 4 5

Not   Exhibited
Exhibited   Consistently

How could you explain the theory of probability simply so an adult learner who is unfamiliar with it might understand it? Or how could you explain an extent scale?

2. Is able to create and use practical   0 1 2 3 4 5
   examples.

If a learner is having a hard time understanding the concept of process, what practical example could you use to explain the concept?

3. Demonstrates respect for and under-   0 1 2 3 4 5
   standing of the adult basic skill learner.

Have you ever worked with an adult learner who was not open to trying to learn and seemed resentful toward the classroom? What do you think was going on for him/her? How did you handle that situation? What was the outcome?

4. Is nondefensive and can accept criticism. 0 1 2 3 4 5

Can you describe a situation when a learner criticized you or what you said, perhaps several times in a row? How did you respond? What was the result? Do you think that was an effective way to manage that situation?

5. Is a good listener.   0 1 2 3 4 5

What are some techniques you might use in a classroom situation to get the learners to give more information and to feel like their viewpoint is understood?

6. Has a positive problem-solving attitude. 0 1 2 3 4 5

Have you ever had a situation occur when you were teaching that was completely out of your control and made it almost impossible to go on teaching at that moment? What occurred and how did you respond to it?

CHARACTERISTICS THAT CAN BE DEVELOPED

Extent Behavior is Exhibited

1. Able to identify learning competency
   requirements in workplace materials.   0 1 2 3 4 5

For this characteristic, select a simple work-related task and ask the candidate to itemize the basic skills required in order to complete the task.

2. Understands the nonacademic
   environment.   0 1 2 3 4 5

Business experience is probably the best indicator for this but you might be able to get an indication by probing for information. Ask the candidate to describe what he or she believes is required for the organization in question to make money and stay competitive.

3. Has the desire and ability to focus
   on identified company training and   0 1 2 3 4 5
   business goals.

You are a new instructor at XYZ company and begin to develop exercises for the curriculum guidelines that have been given to you. You feel strongly that the guidelines are much too narrow and the students first need to improve the grammatical mechanics of their writing and then move on to work-related assignments. What would you do?

fee schedule would be more than competitive with public education. These calculated fees reflected the highest hourly fees of local adult education instructors for classroom hours plus a few hours of preparation.

The instructors that were selected were not certified to teach in public adult education and this was their first experience in workplace training. However, the fee arrangement was satisfactory and even motivating for them. But, their experience with the practical application of the material provided an awareness of both the needs of the learners and the business.

Instructors will develop quickly when they participate in a regular review meeting with the program manager. This review meeting is an informal opportunity for the instructor to express concerns, share success stories, and request materials from the workplace or external sources. Guidelines for this process, including a checklist of data to gather and presentation points to cover, are discussed later. Observations of learner participation levels also can be helpful to the instructor as can occasional conversations between learners and the program manager, either in the classroom or outside, to provide an ongoing evaluation.

Curriculum Designer Selection

Usually, the instructor will also design the curriculum or at least design materials as the program progresses. Sometimes, it is possible to have designers develop part of the materials ahead of time for a base from which to draw. It is helpful for the program manager to have some practical design skills in order to oversee the material development. In order to be able to grow, add, and change with the workplace, it is beneficial to maintain an attitude of willingness to add new material on a just-in-time basis.

If an additional designer is required in order to develop additional material in the beginning of a program, the best ways to find someone with adequate skills for the design of functional material are the following:

- Get a recommendation from someone.

- Assess the skills of the designer being considered by reviewing materials that that person has designed in the past.

• Ask for an example of an exercise that would present one of the needed competencies in a workplace context.

Finally, successful curriculum development does not require a doctorate in instructional design. This level of educational design experience might even be a hindrance if the developer rigidly follows academically accepted models of design at the expense of ignoring business requirements and current quality improvement processes.

Table 17 outlines the critical skills and knowledge required by the role of the curriculum designer.

1C. DEVELOP INSTRUCTORS AND ESTABLISH CONTINUOUS MEASURABLE IMPROVEMENT PROCESSES

Once the instructor has been selected, staff development can begin. The format this takes will be determined by the level of expertise possessed by both the instructor and the program manager. If the training and development experience level of the program manager is not high, consider sending the program manager and the instructors to an offsite train-the-trainer program which emphasizes presentation and facilitation skills, and the delivery of experiential learning.

If the instruction team's participation in a train-the-trainer session is out of the question, the program manager will need to be skilled in all design, implementation, and evaluation areas and be responsible for the development of the rest of the team on a one-on-one basis. The program manager can begin this development by working with the staff on the initial development of materials. For example, at Toro and at Pioneer, I was responsible for program management, staff development, and quality assurance. Another approach would be to develop the program manager in all required areas and give them responsibility for providing initial staff development, managing this staff, and overseeing the ongoing program management.

The program manager should make weekly observations of each class and have a regular meeting time with the instructors in which the following occurs:

- General company and program information is exchanged.
- Feedback on strengths and areas to improve is given.
- Challenges with particular learners are discussed.
- Curriculum ideas and challenges are discussed.
- General support for the instructor is provided.

TABLE 17 Curriculum Designer Selection

Role & Responsibilities	Skills & Knowledge
1. Create work-related exercises in support of training competencies.	1. Understands the workplace or is willing to learn about it and the business goals that drive it.
	2. Can observe a work process and record it in steps.
	3. Can identify the skills required by each step.
	4. Is able to write learning manuals or other communication.
	5. Can simplify complicated work instructions and manufacturing formulas.
	6. Can write clear sequential directions and easy to understand materials.
	7. Can coordinate the development of exercises based on workplace material with skill competencies.
2. Gather information about work processes and needs of the workplace.	1. Has an unobtrusive manner of interacting with organization personnel.
	2. Interviewing skills.
3. Produce clear, work-related master copies of materials.	1. Is computer literate (preferably on the same computer and word processing software that is being used by other instruction team members.)

As a rule of thumb for program managers, class visitation should always include a brief written comment which can be delivered in the weekly meeting. This comment should be about a specific, positive occurrence in the classroom. Areas for instructor growth should be discussed in private with the individual or with the group if it is a common issue. The program manager will be more welcome in the classroom if he or she looks for observations of instructor effectiveness and learner progress on which to comment. A checklist is provided in figure 5.1 to guide the program manager's observations and data collection. This is also an opportunity to collect record-keeping data, which provide another vehicle for evaluating the progress of the program.

Instructor _____ Date _____

YES	NI	Observation or Activity
		Learner involvement.
		Encouraging, problem-solving environment
		Instructor energy level.
		Use of visuals.
		Varied structure of learner participation.
		Clear introduction of new concepts.
		Instructor models TQM behaviors.
		Lesson plan complete for week.
		Competency chart up to date.
		All learners involved.
		No learner dominates.
		Learners know what they are learning.
		COMMENTS

*NI—Needs Improvement

FIGURE 5.1.   **Meeting Checklist for Program Manager and Instructor.**

The program manager is the organization's anchor for the program and the one person who keeps it on track and focused. Presentation style and interaction style are two areas on which the instructor may need feedback from the program manager. Feedback from the program manager on strengths and ways to improve will provide the instructor with support, energy, and focus. Classroom observations should be positive and feedback should be in the form of suggestions for other approaches, acknowledgment of successes, identification of common problems between classes, identification of additions or changes to room arrangement that would be beneficial, and other supportive gestures. Quick interactions between the program manager and the instructor should be mostly positive or problem-solving in nature, never blaming.

If the program manager has training experience, it will be helpful for him or her to present occasionally a demonstration lesson for a concept. This modeling of instruction techniques for instructors can be an effective form of development. This allows the instructor to observe the participants as they interact with the program manager and it may also provide the instructor with new ideas for the instruction of the group.

Another way for an instructor to see other teaching techniques is to observe a strong area of expertise demonstrated by another instructor. This method was very helpful at Pioneer. Because the two instructors on that team had different strengths, they were able to share their talents and learn a lot from each other.

Instructors should be able to look to the program manager and to each other for inspiration, constructive feedback, ideas for improvement, and growth. In this way, the instructors can keep up with the changes in the organization, reflect the current workplace requirements in instructional materials, maintain their focus on competencies, and continue the energy and quality of the BSTQ program.

Instructor development can be facilitated as a team effort. Some of the most effective development comes from shared experiences of the instructional team. Sharing strengths and ideas with each other can be very useful. Instructors need to have a peer group with whom they can interact. They often have people-oriented personality styles. Therefore, they need this interaction in order to refuel their own energies.

Feedback is most effective when it is specific and solicits suggestions for other approaches, acknowledges successes, or identifies common problems between classes. This routine meeting establishes a pattern of involvement and collaboration on the part of the program manager. This communicates that the instructor is not alone. It creates a team approach for the training and encourages the instructor's development in areas that require improvement.

When an opportunity for growth is noted, the program manager can be prepared to demonstrate other approaches or to problem solve with the instructor. If the area that requires improvement is more in the area of interpersonal skills, as in situations that occur in the process of encouraging group participation and feedback, the program manager may need to assume the role of counselor to the participants as well as helper to the instructor.

This type of development is also a good model for the TQM principles. When a person embraces certain attitudes and practices in their own behavior, it is easier to teach that behavior to others. Therefore, instructors who are valued as worthwhile contributors on a team are more likely to treat the program participants as worthwhile contributors. Our behaviors demonstrate our beliefs and philosophy of total quality management, even in the classroom. This is often referred to as "walking the talk."

THE TORO COMPANY

When we began at Toro, I had only ideas about where to find instructors for the basic skills program, so I had to do considerable research. I looked for all of the local institutions that might be in contact with instructors of adults, including the two local community colleges, Riverside Community College and Valley Community College in San Bernardino, California. I also visited a public adult education facility in the area to observe what they were doing and to get recommendations for instructors who might be available to work in the Toro program. The staff and faculty were cordial and helpful. They were especially interested in working with local businesses. I spoke with one of their instructors who was implementing a training program in one of the Riverside companies. When he began to show me the books he would use, I knew we had different perceptions of workplace basic skills training. These books were textbooks in which I saw no indication of functional workplace curriculum design efforts. Additionally, our conversation indicated that he had heard the term total quality management but possessed only a beginning awareness of the concept.

The superintendent of this adult education facility provided me with the names of instructors who might be available for the positions at Toro. He had been helpful and seemed to truly want to work with local businesses on adult education issues. It seemed to me, however, that there was a large gap between what they were able to offer and what was needed for a successful program at Toro.

Back at Toro, I discovered that all of the substitute teachers, including some community college instructors, were registered with the California State Employment Development Department (EDD). Several calls to that office communicating the need for a quick response produced more instructor candidates. I also scheduled interviews with one or two instructors referred by the adult school as I continued searching for other candidates.

Among the respondents from these sources, three stand out. One came to the interview unprofessionally dressed. However, she seemed to care about her students, was quite understanding of them, and wanted them to like her. When I indicated that she would be producing classroom exercises using workplace material, she began to get uneasy. During the interview, it became clear she would not be comfortable without a textbook as a basis for instruction. The assignment at Toro would require the instructor to function without a regular textbook and to create instructional lessons from the work situations. Table 18 lists some of the positive and negative characteristics of this first candidate.

TABLE 18 Candidate #1

Positive Characteristics	Negative Characteristics
Empathic toward learners.	Tendency to be too easy going.
Kind and encouraging approach.	No skills in designing functional materials.
Certified to teach adult education.	Unprofessional appearance.

TABLE 19 Candidate #2

Positive Characteristics	Negative Characteristics
Knowledgeable in linguistics.	No evidence of practical application ability.
Graduate degree.	Possibly too academic or theoretical.
Well traveled, experienced with different cultures.	No experience teaching in business.

The second candidate was highly qualified with at least a masters degree in linguistics. He had worked with several different cultures and languages, was well traveled, and was experienced at developing exercises. Although he was experienced and educated, he seemed to be too academically oriented to be effective as a basic skills instructor, as it required a practical approach to instruction. We needed an instructor to whom the participants could relate. Table 19 shows a comparison of the second candidate's major strengths and weaknesses.

Implementation at Toro was scheduled to begin in two weeks and we still did not have an instructor. Then, one of my calls to the EDD office paid off; a community college Spanish instructor came in for an interview. I described the difference between teaching Spanish and what we wanted him to do at Toro. He was especially confident in his ability to develop exercises from workplace material. He had developed similar material for students in his Spanish classes. As he described the material he developed for his students, he described the functional design skills for which we were looking. He was motivated and enthusiastic. He had some knowledge of the population to be trained, and he had a practical, application-oriented approach to developing exercises from work materials, although he had no formal instructor or design training.

This man was hired as the first instructor for basic skills training at Toro. While there were some characteristics of this instructor that were less than ideal, he had some critical positive characteristics as described in Table 20.

Having always worked in an academic setting, he was quite protective of his classroom and at times had to be reminded that Toro was not in the training business. It was difficult for him to

TABLE 20 Candidate #3

Positive Characteristics	Negative Characteristics
Was able to develop work-related materials that supported the basic skills competencies.	Protective of his territory, tended to be defensive.
Could simplify difficult concepts.	Tended to act as if his classroom were the center of the business.
Encouraged and pushed the learners.	Had slightly superior attitude.
Created a safe place for learners in the classroom.	Had difficulty sharing the spotlight.
Was certified to teach adults.	

internalize the concept that Toro Irrigation made and sold sprinklers and training was a support for the business goals. It was difficult for him to be nondefensive when interrupted, flexible when there were changes in schedule, or accommodating when double scheduling of rooms occurred. In addition, he had a difficult time working with another instructor who was brought in later and never quite mastered the art of being a team player. I spent a lot of program management time working on this concept with him, and although it got better, it never went away.

The strengths and weaknesses of this instructor are mentioned here because, even though his opportunities for growth were considerable, his performance in the classroom and his ability to relate workplace materials to basic skills training were very good. He was qualified to teach in the community college by means of a degree in a specific area. Although he did not have all of the desired critical job qualifications, the ones he had were important and difficult to find. His performance required the extensive involvement of the program manager in order to minimize interpersonal conflicts. Even with these areas of weakness, his strengths added greatly to the training program's success.

At Toro, we included the BSTQ instructors in an on-site train-the-trainer class in design and development that was customized for Toro. In addition, a class in facilitation and presentation was presented by Marla Bradley of Bradley, Lambert, Steele

Associates of Los Angeles. This class included other organization personnel who had training responsibilities.

The training's value to the BSTQ trainers was threefold. The BSTQ trainers built credibility for themselves in the organization by being exposed to the same training as the other trainers, the BSTQ trainers learned more about the organization issues in training, and the BSTQ trainers were able to do informal networking with organization personnel.

PIONEER ELECTRONICS TECHNOLOGY, INC. (PET)

At Pioneer, we were fortunate again because we were able to draw upon trainers who had experience at Toro and had benefited from development in that program. By the time they were involved in the Pioneer training, they knew what was expected for the classroom atmosphere and training philosophy. There was also a high level of trust among us that allowed for even more intense development of their skills. This left us free to concentrate on the customization of the program for the Pioneer environment.

The instructors had developed excellent skills in two different areas. One was quite proficient in teaching flowcharts, process analysis, and supervisory skills. The other instructor was highly skilled in working with ESL learners. Both were good at developing learner self-confidence and competence. They often turned to each other for advice and coaching in a particular situation where the other instructor was the expert. This cross training of instructors provided Pioneer with an excellent instruction team capable of working with the diverse groups that went through BSTQ training.

The variety of competencies that the instructors had to be sensitive to included the following:

- Preliterate and extremely low ESL skills (in the same group) at the time of the participants' entry into ESL group attended ESL before entering BSTQ.

- Low English skills but some literacy in Spanish at the time of entry into ESL; [attended ESL before entering BSTQ.]

- Intermediate English skills; low literacy in Spanish; literacy in Asian language if appropriate; [attended ESL before entering BSTQ.]

- Advanced English skills; literate in Spanish or Asian language; low math skills; no ESL training.
- Lead production employees with strong ability to learn; few English skills; low math skills; mixed skill group; no ESL training prior to BSTQ.

Structured tools for charting progress and maintaining communication within the instructional team were developed for Pioneer. These tools included a competency grid. The competency grid created a living record of program focus. Each class day the competencies which were covered that day were checked on the grid. With this tool I could tell which competencies each group had covered and which were being overlooked. The instructors also liked it as a tracking tool.

These tools provided consistency and stability to the regular interface between the program manager and instructors, and PET management. This process of structured, regular interaction resulted in more support for the instructors than we had at Toro, more focus on competencies which encouraged better coverage of competencies, and more accountability of the instruction team to the client.

SUMMARY OF IMPORTANT POINTS

- Begin the selection of the instructional team early in the planning process.
- The program manager will be responsible for assuring development of the instructors and facilitating ongoing feedback.
- Do not eliminate instructor candidates for lack of formal instructor training or certification.
- Train instructors before beginning the program and continue development for the duration of the program.
- Provide instructors with ongoing developmental feedback and include them in weekly staff meetings where they can interact with other instructors.

IDENTIFY THE CURRICULUM AND COMPETENCIES, AND ESTABLISH A TRACKING SYSTEM

Step 2: Identify Curriculum, Competencies, and Establish a Tracking System

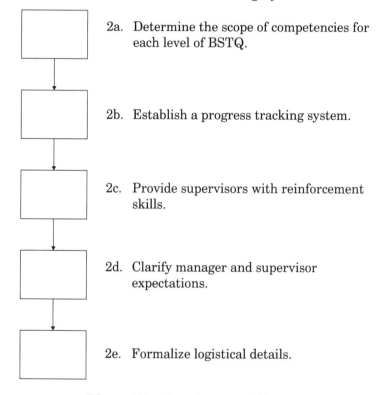

2a. Determine the scope of competencies for each level of BSTQ.

2b. Establish a progress tracking system.

2c. Provide supervisors with reinforcement skills.

2d. Clarify manager and supervisor expectations.

2e. Formalize logistical details.

Phase II—Development Process

The second step of Phase II, Identify the Curriculum and Competencies, and Establish a Tracking System, consists of the above five interrelated parts.

At this point in the development phase, it is necessary to narrow the focus for the BSTQ training program. During the discovery phase, a large amount of data was gathered and analyzed in several ways. These activities included the following:

- Focus groups were conducted.

- TQM materials were analyzed.

- Company goals were clarified.

- ESL assessment was conducted, if required.

- Basic skills written assessment was conducted.

- Major gaps in skill requirements and abilities were analyzed.

With the data gathering, and the first step of the development phase—instructor selection—completed, the specific competencies can be determined and the curriculum finalized so that lesson and material development can begin.

2A. DETERMINE THE SCOPE OF COMPETENCIES FOR EACH LEVEL OF BSTQ

The content of BSTQ training materials can either simplify the total quality management training materials selected by your organization or it can develop quality improvement process skills in a work-related context. Learning skills can be developed with either of these approaches. The question to ask is, "What do we expect the participants to be able to do when they enter the quality improvement training or when they participate in a quality improvement team? What skills will they need in order to contribute to the ISO 9000 certification process?" In other words, what knowledge and skills are employees expected to bring with them to the quality improvement training and activities? The answers to this question should comprise the minimum content for the BSTQ program.

Depending on the skill level of the workforce, these minimum competencies will probably include the most basic reading, writing, math, and study skills. These are the skills that many of us assume every adult has mastered. It is easy to forget that not everyone has had the good fortune to enjoy a strong educational background plus further development at work.

You may have an overwhelming amount of data at this point. You may also be struck with the desire to remedy all of the education deficiencies of the workforce with the training program you are about to develop and implement. Resist this urge. Organizations are not in business to replace the public education system. Organizational training programs must be focused on skills and knowledge that directly impact the work and the organizational goals.

Plan for Success

A common mistake that practitioners new to identifying sequenced competencies make is the creation of competencies that sound good but are much too ambitious to achieve. It is important to remember that the goal is not the assessment or a list of unrealistic competencies to be achieved. The goal is improved basic workplace skills to support total quality management implementation. The competencies should describe a sequence of specific basic skills that will increase employee ability to support TQM.

The competencies are a road map for BSTQ. They keep the instruction on track but they do not describe all of the activities and scenery along the way. It is critical that these competencies are ones that can be achieved successfully by participants. Create a realistic list of competencies for which you, as program manager or a member of the instruction team, can accept accountability. In other words, only commit to competencies with which the training, considering all the variables, can be undeniably successful. This puts the focus on the learning process where it should be.

Once the most critical skills required for achievement of the organization's business goals have been identified, (ISO 9000 certification, reengineering, total quality management, or excellence in customer service) review these skills again and divide them into the two levels described in chapter 3. When this is accomplished, look at the list again and perform an analysis of required skills.

The following is an analysis of the required skills that identify specific competencies:

1. Go over the list you created in chapter 3 and put the skills in order from the simplest to the most complex (see Table 25).

2. Use this process to identify more than one layer of skills.

3. Describe the specific skills that must be acquired to successfully perform each of the identified skills.

4. Arrange the basic skills in sequential order so that each category is built from the most basic to the most complex skill.

Working Within the Time Frame

The time constraints of workplace training require a focus on only the "must know" skills from this list. This training will probably consist of 40 to 48 total hours, delivered in two-hour sessions twice a week for 10 to 12 weeks. There may be two repetitions of this 40- to 48-hour class. If repeated twice, the total amount of time in the classroom will only amount to two or three weeks of eight-hour days, the normal format for full-time education. For this reason, the sessions must be very focused on the most needed and basic skills.

For each of the major categories of skills, choose no more than 10 (preferably fewer) of the most basic skills. If there are not many skills in a category, select three to five. For example, if the task is to describe defects accurately in writing, the first thing that may have to be learned is vocabulary and the next may be word order and sentence structure. In some extreme cases, the first skill may be writing the English alphabet.

One approach to this task is to look at the list and ask, "If the learners can only master 10 specific skills from the largest categories on this list (probably written communication and math), which 10 would they need to learn first?", and "Which skills are most essential for achieving the organizational goal?" With this approach you can focus in on the necessary competencies rather than try to include all the knowledge an employee must have to be considered educated in English or math.

Be realistic about how many skills can be developed in 40 hours. The first level of skills will represent minimum essential knowledge that must be in place. Skills that had been in level 1 originally may have to wait until level 2. Use the same process to select each of the next layers of skills. This process encourages focus on essential knowledge and skills and provides a set of competencies that can guide the curriculum development. These competencies will be the focus of instruction and the yardstick for measurement.

Another simple task that may be helpful is to create an instructional calendar and distribute the competencies from the list over the projected time period. This will create a preliminary lesson schedule that will provide a means of more accurately judging that the competencies you have selected will fit the designated time frame. This is not a final schedule. This is just a check of the possibility of covering the competencies within the designated time frame.

2B. ESTABLISH A PROGRESS TRACKING SYSTEM

When the competencies and the levels of BSTQ have been identified, construct a grid to record the presentation and the review of competencies. This gives the program manager and the instructor a visual representation of which competencies are covered often and which ones are not touched on at all.

It is quite easy for an instructor to continue emphasizing a topic because he or she thinks it's worthwhile. The formal competencies and the tracking grids keep the contract with the customer visible at all times.

A brief lesson plan can be prepared in which the instructors identify the competencies that are being developed for each class and the exercises that will be used for developing those competencies. These lesson plans and competency grids allow any member of the instruction team—instructor, program manager, or internal contact—to instantly see where the gaps in training occur. This information can be used to answer the following questions:

- What competency doesn't fit here? (Sometimes a competency proves to be inappropriate and does not fit in a sequence with the rest of the competencies.)

- If a competency doesn't fit, should it be included in the next level or dropped from the curriculum?

- Which competencies need better structured lessons, planning, or materials?

- Are we overlooking any of the competencies in planning our lesson?

- Is a particular area of instruction being focused on too long?

This method of tracking progress on the competency grids also strengthens the accountability of the program management and instruction teams. It is simple and does not require excessive paperwork from the instructors. This step, tracking progress, can be used as a checkpoint for what is being accomplished with each group to assure quality on a weekly basis. As competencies are reviewed and accomplishments discussed by the instructor and program manager, adjustments can be made in materials or classroom exercises as needed. Using this method, which represents the check mode of the PDCA cycle, the instruction team can adjust material, content, or style in order to get back on track rather than wait until the end of a session to discover it has come up lacking. If getting back on track is not feasible with the group in question, the instruction team can inform the supervisors ahead of evaluation time and ask for input from them.

This type of tracking makes it possible to maintain the program focus even when we add content at the request of production supervisors. Another benefit is the ability to review a specific group's progress accurately at any given time. When several groups are in training at the same time, the ability to pinpoint a particular group's progress is critical to a successful program implementation.

2C. PROVIDE SUPERVISORS WITH REINFORCEMENT SKILLS

Analyzing the responses to the question, "What would you like your managers to do better?" provides some insight into the management development that will be required for the success of the BSTQ program. The skills listed by both supervisors and employees in response to this question are almost entirely communication and leadership skills. Technical skills were not included in the responses. This focus on people management skills needing improvement is typical of recent research information on skill deficiencies that contribute to management failure. Among these studies is a report by Michael Lombardo and Cynthis D. McCauley, *The Dynamics of Management Derailment,* published by the Center for Creative Leadership in Greensboro, North Carolina in 1988.

When this need for improved supervisory and management skills exists, it is especially important to clarify this group's role in the success of the BSTQ training. It is also important to begin supervisor and management training as soon as possible. If this training does not occur before or concurrently with the BSTQ training, the managers and supervisors may not be prepared to respond to the learners with appropriate supportive responses. In this case, the program management team will need to provide supervisors and managers with information regarding supportive versus nonsupportive behaviors.

The second focus group that is conducted with supervisors and managers provides the program manager an opportunity to:

- Clarify the supportive role of the supervisor in the BSTQ training's success.

- Define supportive supervisory behaviors.

- Provide examples of supportive behaviors.

The program manager should take advantage of every opportunity to meet with these supervisory and management groups. A constant flow of communication about the training is absolutely necessary in order for the members of this group to feel involved and informed. Follow up the meetings with a written summary, if possible. This is the third step of the well-known presentation guide:

1. Tell them what you're going to tell them.

2. Tell them.

3. Tell them what you told them.

The second focus group with supervisors and managers may include the following steps:

1. Review data gathering to date.

2. Use the following data to clarify expectations of supervisors and managers.
   - This is what you said you wanted.
   - This is what TQM will require.
   - This is what can be done if we hold two-hour classes twice per week for two 10-week sessions.
   - Is there anything we have left out that you think is critical?

3. Clarify leadership role.
   - Introduce LEAD concept as a way of emphasizing supervisor and manager role as follows:
     - Listen.
     - Encourage.
     - Ask.
     - Demonstrate.

LEAD Concepts for Supervisors and Managers

The sooner managers and supervisors can present the LEAD ideas to the supervisors and managers, the more opportunity there will be to encourage their support and involvement of the program.

Listen: It is going to be very important that you, as managers and supervisors, listen carefully to the participants as they practice their new skills. From time to time, the program manager will update you on the content of the classes so you can reinforce particular learning. This is a perfect opportunity to reinforce desired behaviors such as speaking up about a problem on the line. The behavior to be reinforced is speaking up. Even if the information is not important, the behavior is. Always keep in mind the behaviors you're looking for and reinforce them. The response might be something like, "That particular defect is within specified limits so it does not have to be rejected, but I'm really glad you saw it and pointed it out. That's exactly what we need you to do!"

Do not respond by saying, "That defect isn't serious so we don't need to identify it." The latter statement will discourage the employee from speaking up again.

Encourage: Encourage employee participation in the training by planning ahead so their work responsibilities are covered and allow them to go to class. When new classes are started, talk about how worthwhile the training is and how supervisors and managers have helped determine the curriculum. Never put down the program or the participants. Supervisor support is critical to the success of the program. Be involved; visit the classroom so you know first hand what is going on. Encourage participants by recognizing new behaviors and efforts. Those of us who have more than the basic skills can be secure enough to give positive feedback to others for having the courage to try.

Ask: Ask the participants what they are learning and if there is any way you can support them. Is there anything they would like to practice with you or with other employees? Ask the instructor what is happening in class and if there is anything you can do to support the learning. If you don't understand why a concept is being presented in the classroom, ask.

Demonstrate: Demonstrate your support of the program by all of the actions just mentioned and by trying to be a better communicator. Read about supervisory communication. Ask the participants to demonstrate what they learned so you can try it. Model a learning, problem-solving attitude.

2D. CLARIFY MANAGER AND SUPERVISOR EXPECTATIONS

The second focus group meeting is also an opportunity to clarify how the manager and supervisor groups will evaluate the training program. Determining this evaluation criteria up front helps to provide focus for the training curriculum and models the customer focus that is a fundamental aspect of any quality initiative. These groups are important internal customers for the training. From this information the program manager can identify areas where progress should be communicated to managers and supervisors on an ongoing basis, both formally and informally. In clarifying this criteria, be prepared to present a visual of the criteria and verify that this is the direction the training should take. This information provides an initial basis for communicating progress.

Give this feedback, summarize the meeting in writing, and then expect to refer back to this feedback session when evaluating the training. There is a tendency for performance expectations to increase as a program is accepted and integrated into daily activities. This phenomena is an example of Golembiewski's theories of alpha, beta, and gamma changes as applied by Mohrman and Novelli[1] to changes in office automation systems. It can also be applied to BSTQ training programs.

Alpha Change Stage

At first, a new system is exciting but confusing because we don't understand its capabilities. People expecting an alpha change expect a change in the levels of output while the criteria for evaluating the output remain the same. In a BSTQ program, many people in the organization find the dedication of resources exciting and promising, agreeing that increasing basic skills will enhance the implementation of total quality. However, these same individuals are still evaluating employees informally against the same criteria as they were before total quality implementation. Examples of these criteria include the following:

- Do employees still speak a language other than English on the line?

- Are employees filling out labor cards correctly?

- Do employees speak up when they do not understand?

Beta Change Stage

A beta change refers to situations where the direction and type of output remain the same but the criteria or the scales used to measure outputs change. In information systems, one might expect the technology to produce output that once was considered high and would now be considered moderate. The technology would bring with it a new standard for output evaluation, although the kind of output may remain essentially the same. In a BSTQ program, this beta stage exists when an organization's su-

---

1. Mohrman, A.M. and Luke Novelli, Jr. *Three Types of Change in the Automated Office.* University of Southern California, Graduate School of Business Administration, The Center for Effective Organizations. 1983, p. 1–2.

pervisors and managers accept classes that take place regularly and recognize the use of resources to cover the work responsibilities of employees in training. They begin to add content to the curriculum, increase their expectations of skills to be developed, and possibly take the progress that has been made for granted.

Gamma Change Stage

A gamma change reflects changes in reality and the world view so that activities before and after the change are not directly comparable. Not only are the activities done in different ways because of the technology, but they also seem different in nature and are therefore evaluated in different ways.[2] According to Mohrman, the original criteria for evaluating success has changed. What would have been extraordinary performance before, becomes ordinary now. In the BSTQ program, meeting the original performance goals becomes commonplace, and supervisory or management personnel tend to look to BSTQ to solve their own management issues. There may be requests to use classroom time for supervisors to fill out forms or educate participants about some company issue. Such training uses scarce classroom time and must facilitate the development of identified competencies, or the program will be off course. After classes have been in session for several months, the organization may forget that the same curriculum is being taught over and over to different groups. There may be a tendency to want to add concepts to the curriculum beyond the original design.

When adequate records of the original list of expectations and their revisions are kept, then it is possible to refer to the original expectations as a source of evaluation. Meeting additional expectations not defined in the beginning may cause other competencies to be overlooked. The program manager must be realistic about accomplishing the original goals when additional organizational tasks are requested to be handled in BSTQ class. On several occasions, the BSTQ case study instructors guided learners through new health insurance forms, ride share forms, and numerous other tasks. Once, the program manager received a request to test the clarity of a new retirement plan as presented in literature and video. This request was denied because

---

2. Ibid.

it would have interrupted the flow of the curriculum and been disruptive to the success of the program. Organizations appreciate this type of candor from the program manager because it assures them they can request changes, and if these changes are inappropriate, given the overall goals of the BSTQ training program, they will not be implemented.

2E. FORMALIZE LOGISTICAL DETAILS

There are some minimum guidelines for adult education that have proven to be successful for the BSTQ programs. The first has to do with class length. I have found the most efficient use of time is to conduct classes in two-hour blocks. Employees who are not used to being in class for long lengths of time will not be able to sit for more than two hours, and supervisors will not want to release them for more than two hours. In fact, most managers will suggest one-hour classes. The program manager must maintain a strong position on this. One-hour classes waste time shifting employees to and from the line. It takes a few minutes to get individual thoughts focused on the classroom, and just when the class is gaining momentum, it's time to leave again. If you encounter a consultant who tells you they can provide worthwhile training in thirty-minute segments, your antennae should go up as you sense the atmosphere for other signs of a lack of training expertise.

The class should meet twice a week for continuity and reinforcement of learning. Three times a week would be ideal (especially for ESL), but try not to have unreasonable expectations. The following chart shows approximate start and stop months for each of eight groups of 11 to 13 participants. Columns two and three show the days on which the groups attend class. This schedule assumes that one training room and one instructor are available.

The next scheduling decision has to do with the number of basic skill levels to develop and the number of session repetitions in each basic skill level. In other words, should there be one or two levels (or more) of basic skills, and how many sessions should there be in each level?

Programs longer than 10 or 12 weeks are not recommended. If a class meets twice per week for 10 weeks, each participant is

TABLE 21 Sample Schedule for 90 Employees

96 hours of BSTQ training delivered in 48-hour segments, two-hours, twice per week for 12 weeks.

Class	M&W	T&TH	12 Wks Jan–Mar	12 Wks Apr–Jn	12 Wks July–Sept	12 Wks Oct–Dec
Group 1	x		xxxxxxx	xxxxxxx		
Group 2	x		xxxxxxx	xxxxxxx		
Group 3	x		xxxxxxx	xxxxxxx		
Group 4		x	xxxxxxx	xxxxxxx		
Group 5		x	xxxxxxx	xxxxxxx		
Group 6		x	xxxxxxx	xxxxxxx		
Group 7	x				xxxxxxx	xxxxxxx
Group 8	x				xxxxxxx	xxxxxxx

in training for 40 hours. If the class meets twice per week for 12 weeks, each participant is in training for 48 hours. Everyone, supervisors and employees, needs a sense of completion and celebration at regular intervals.

Another element to consider is the number of participants in each class. An ideal number is between 9 and 15 participants, depending on the abilities of the group. The following information regarding class size needs to be clarified:

- The number of employees that can be off the lines or the floor at a given time.
- The maximum class size for effective training given the available rooms.
- The number of classes that can be in session at a given time.
- The number of months it will take to complete the training using that class size and that number of classes.

Therefore, if there are 90 employees who will attend BSTQ and BSTQ consists of two sessions, each 12 weeks long, the length of the training for each group of employees will be 24 weeks or 6 months. If there is only one training room and you train three classes on Monday and Wednesday and three classes on Tuesday and Thursday, 72 employees can finish in six months. Then you would need to have another round of training for two classes of nine people. This schedule provides for no more than 12 employees to be off the line at any given time, and the training will be completed in one year (see Table 22). The reality is that most organizations have a difficult time allowing over seven percent of the workforce to be in class at any given time.

Both Toro and Pioneer made a commitment to cover production personnel requirements by planning for temporaries to cover positions on the lines. At Toro, the general manager was completely committed to the success of the training, and at Pioneer, the president was equally committed to the program. This commitment is a very strong playing card when production pressures increase. Supervisors will naturally look at the temporary cancellation of training as a quick way to ease the stress of increased production demands. When the executive backs the program with both action and a budget for temporary help, supervisors will find other ways to manage production.

THE TORO COMPANY

At Toro, the reading and writing basic skill requirements centered around understanding how to fill out specific forms and how to interpret company communication. Description of defects and specific process steps were also important issues. In the basic skill competencies for Toro and Pioneer (see tables 23 and 24), Toro's reading and writing competencies focus more on specific forms and communications than do Pioneer's. Pioneer's requirements encompassed basic work vocabulary and behaviors for understanding and being understood.

At Toro, the competencies were used as a guide for curriculum development and implementation. They were not part of a formal communication between the instructor and the program manager. In the early classes, this lack of communication allowed the instructor to go too deeply into some areas such as long division of decimals and multiplication of mixed fractions. While this diversion from the guidelines did no harm, it took

TABLE 22 Logistical Factors Effecting Program Structure, Duration, and Cost

Class	Effect on Organization
Class size for best instruction (7–12).	Smaller classes lengthen the program, requiring more rounds of training. Small classes ease the impact of production coverage (fewer people out at one time.)
Dedicated training room of the appropriate size.	Each training room will be lost to the organization for the duration of the training. Rooms cannot be switched for larger group meetings.
Two-hour sessions.	Supervisors have to adjust mental models of training from one-hour information delivery to two-hour interactive sessions. Requires job coverage.
Repeated twice per week.	Must plan ahead to cover jobs. Plan to budget costs for coverage.
Continued 10 to 12 weeks. Allows for repetition and completion of competencies.	Must accept that, even when production is heavy, schedule is maintained.
Implementation length of program depends on the following: • Total number to be trained. • Class size. • Number of classrooms available. • Number of classes in session simultaneously. • Number of people off the floor at one time. • Number of sessions per BSTQ level. • Unplanned interruptions to schedule.	Implementation length of program means the following: • Resources allocated to cover jobs while trainees are in class for a considerable length of time. • Trainees are not available to assist in covering business requirements during high-production or high-pressure situations. • Indirect labor costs increase; more difficult to achieve efficiency goals.
Instructors available to cover odd-hour shifts.	Larger numbers of second- and third-shift employees may have to attend at the same time due to infrequency of accommodating classes.

TABLE 23 Toro Irrigation Basic Skills Competencies

Reading, Writing, Speaking

1.0 Job Knowledge
  1.1 Read and interpret signs, posters, and printed announcements.
  1.2 Read, understand, and use work-related vocabulary.
  1.3 Read and understand job descriptions and job opportunity information.
  1.4 Read and understand information about training opportunities.
  1.5 Read and interpret employee handbooks.
  1.6 Read and interpret company memos and announcements.
  1.7 Read and interpret information found in company and local newspapers, periodicals, etc.
  1.8 Read and interpret standard and daily written job instructions.
  1.9 Read and interpret information about wages, deductions, and benefits including forms, pamphlets, memos, and charts.
  1.10 Read, interpret, and complete simple job-related forms.
  1.11 Interpret job responsibilities and performance reviews.
  1.12 Read, interpret, and record descriptions of job processes.

2.0 Interpersonal Communication Skills
  2.1 Describe a problem situation with work processes on interpersonal issues.
  2.2 Give feedback, both positive and constructive.
  2.3 Present an idea orally and on paper.
  2.4 Speak up, say no, risk rejection.
  2.5 Ask questions.
  2.6 Listen for information and understand other viewpoints.
  2.7 Clarify and check to make sure you have the right information.
  2.8 Follow spoken, sequential directions.

3.0 Graphics
  3.1 Read and interpret graphs, tables, charts, and spreadsheets.
  3.2 Interpret pictures including job processes, maps, posters, and cartoons.
  3.3 Use graphics to explain, support, or represent an idea.

4.0 General Life Experience
  4.1 Understand concepts of time.
    4.1.1 Interpret clock time.
    4.1.2 Identify months of the year and the days of the week.
  4.2 Use community agencies and services.
    4.2.1 Identify educational services and how to use them.
    4.2.2 Interpret information about educational opportunities found in publications.

TABLE 24 Toro Irrigation Basic Skills Competencies

MATH

1.0 Counting.

2.0 Comparing and ordering numbers.
  2.1 Meaning of <, >, =.
  2.2 Number lines.

3.0 Compute using whole numbers.
  3.1 Simple addition using whole numbers.
  3.2 Simple addition using whole numbers with renaming (carrying).
  3.3 Simple subtraction using whole numbers.
  3.4 Simple subtraction using whole numbers with renaming.
  3.5 Multiply with one digit multipliers.
  3.6 Multiply with one digit multipliers with renaming.
  3.7 Multiply with two digit multipliers.
  3.8 Simple division.
  3.9 Division with remainder.
  3.10 Two-digit quotient.
  3.11 Compute averages.
  3.12 Compute ranges.

4.0 Compute using decimals.
  4.1 Add using decimals.
  4.2 Subtract using decimals.
  4.3 Multiply using decimals.
  4.4 Figure percentages.
  4.5 Writing percentages as decimals and decimals as percentages.
  4.6 Compute discounts.
  4.7 Divide using decimals.

5.0 Compute using fractions.
  5.1 Changing fractions to mixed numbers.
  5.2 Adding fractions.
  5.3 Subtracting fractions.

6.0 Use weights, measures, measurement scales.
  6.1 Interpret graphs.
  6.2 Select, compute, or interpret appropriate standard measurements as required.

more than its share of time so that other critical areas did not receive the emphasis they needed. This was discovered in the first sessions, and new effort was focused on staying on track.

The competencies at Toro were never officially divided into two skill levels, but were approached as one set of competencies to be achieved in two sessions of basic skills training. After the first groups went through training, the point where the competencies divided into two fairly distinct levels became more clear.

The extent of the basic skill competency training developed for the Toro program required two sessions of basic skills. This provided a sense of completion at the end of the first session and contributed to individual motivation. The two levels of training at Toro consisted of courses of 12 weeks each with two sessions per week, or 48 hours.

Since Toro, had a large workforce and a large group of BSTQ participants, they were able to run two classes at once, sometimes four sessions per day. They operated in three shifts and required an early class (6:30 a.m. to 8:30 a.m.) for the third shift, and later a 5:00 p.m.-to-7:00 p.m. class for the second shift.

PIONEER ELECTRONICS TECHNOLOGY, INC. (PET)

Several different curricula were developed for PET, although one set of competencies, as identified in Tables 25 and 26, was used. The reasons for this were the following:

- Each facility manufactured a different product. One facility produced large screen TV's and one facility produced speaker cabinets.

- Levels of ESL proficiency varied from not literate in any language to very verbal and well educated.

- The supervisors and leads needed a different focus for their curriculum than did the other employees.

- A curriculum to support other business goals for supervisor development was created and implemented. This required additional competencies.

The content of lessons at PET changed with each group so that curriculum development was ongoing.

A tool for tracking competencies, the competency grid, was developed for the Pioneer program to visually display those

**TABLE 25 Pioneer Electronics Technology, Inc.
BASIC WORKPLACE SKILLS CURRICULUM**

LEVEL 1	LEVEL 2
READING, WRITING	**READING, WRITING**
1.0 Job-Related Reading and Writing	**1.0 Job-Related Reading and Writing**
1.1 Read and interpret signs, safety posters.	1.1 Read and interpret signs, posters, and printed announcements.
1.2 Read, understand, use, and write work-related vocabulary (simple words, 2 or 3 word phrases).	1.2 Read, understand, use, and write work-related vocabulary (1-to-4-syllable words, 3-to-5-word phrases).
1.3 Read and write simple safety instructions.	1.3 Read, interpret, and record job-related safety instructions and appropriate responses.
1.4 Read and find information listed in alphabetical order.	1.4 Use text organizers to sequence main points and locate information.
1.5 Read and interpret standard and daily written job instructions.	1.5 Identify specific job situations for application of information.
1.6 Read, interpret, and complete simple job-related forms.	1.6 Read, interpret, and complete required job-related forms.
1.7 Read, interpret, discuss, and list steps in job processes.	1.7 Read, interpret, and record descriptions of job processes in proper sequence.
1.8 Record date, time, and other simple information on charts and graphs.	1.8 Record date, time, and other data on forms, charts, and graphs.
1.9 Write simple communications.	1.9 State and write short descriptions of problems and simple communications.
	1.10 Read and interpret short descriptions of problems.

(continued)

127

TABLE 25 Continued

LEVEL 1	LEVEL 2
READING, WRITING (continued)	**READING, WRITING (continued)**
2.0 Interpersonal Communication Skills	**2.0 Interpersonal Communication Skills**
2.1 Follow and give verbal instructions.	2.1 Follow verbal, sequential instructions beginning with sets of three and progressing.
2.2 Describe specific behaviors in a problem situation or work process.	2.2 Describe specific behavior in a problem situation or work process.
2.3 Describe specific behavior in a problem situation or interpersonal issue.	2.3 Describe specific behavior in a problem situation or interpersonal issue.
2.4 Ask questions.	2.4 Ask questions to get information.
2.5 Listen for specific information (e.g., instructions).	2.5 Listen for specific information (e.g., instructions).
2.6 Clarify to make sure information is correct.	2.6 Describe possible solutions to work process problems.
	2.7 Clarify to make sure understanding is correct.
3.0 Use of Graphics at Work	**3.0 Use of Graphics at Work**
3.1 Begin to read and interpret graphs and tables.	3.1 Read and interpret graphs, tables, charts, and spreadsheets.
3.2 Read and identify up to three items on schematics, drawings, and maps.	3.2 Read, interpret, and construct more than three items on schematics, drawings, and maps.
3.3 Use graphs to record learning progress.	3.3 Use graphs to record and display data.
3.4 Interpret pictures including job processes, maps, and posters.	3.4 Construct simple process flow diagrams.

(continued)

TABLE 25 Continued

LEVEL 1	LEVEL 2
READING, WRITING (continued)	**READING, WRITING (continued)**
4.0 Learning and Study Skills	**4.0 Learning and Study Skills**
4.1 Apply techniques of setting learning goals.	4.1 Identify individual learning goals and action steps.
4.2 Read for specific information.	4.2 Read for specific information.
4.3 Identify whether you have the right resource.	4.3 Skim for overview information.
4.4 Find job-related information in manuals and other resources.	4.4 Find job-related information in manuals and other resources.
4.5 Formulate questions as a learning tool.	4.5 Formulate questions as a learning tool.
4.6 Identify and summarize important points.	4.6 Identify and summarize important points.
4.7 Use specific skills to increase test performance.	4.7 Use specific skills to increase test performance.
4.8 Use resources to seek information (e.g., dictionaries, handbooks).	4.8 Use resources to seek information (e.g., dictionaries, telephone directories, postage charts, labels, handbooks, manuals).
4.9 Recognize and use different sections of resource materials (e.g., index).	4.9 Recognize and use different sections of resource materials (e.g., index, glossary, chapter headings, etc.).
5.0 Critical Thinking and Problem-Solving Skills	**5.0 Critical Thinking and Problem-Solving Skills**
5.1 Identify similarities and differences in a variety of concrete objects.	5.1 Identify similarities and differences in a variety of situations and relationships.
5.2 Practice the skills required to sort and classify.	5.2 Practice the skills required to differentiate, sort, and classify information.
5.3 Demonstrate ability to identify logical results ("If this happens, then the possible results would be . . .")	5.3 Demonstrate ability to creatively identify possibilities.
5.4 Participate appropriately in problem-solving, brainstorming, discussing, contributing to discussion.	5.4 Participate appropriately in problem-solving, brainstorming, discussing, contributing to discussion.
5.5 Logically identify relationships between objects, as in simple analogies.	5.5 Identify similarities and differences in a variety of
	5.6 Identify alternative solutions and consequences.

**TABLE 26 Pioneer Electronics Technology, Inc.
BASIC WORKPLACE SKILLS CURRICULUM**

LEVEL 1	LEVEL 2
MATH	**MATH**
1.0 Numbers	
1.1 Accurately count number of objects in ones, tens, and hundreds.	
1.2 Determine differences in sequence of digits.	
1.3 Differentiate <, >, =.	
1.4 Place quantities on number lines.	
1.5 Demonstrate understanding of place value.	
2.0 Compute using whole numbers	**2.0 Compute using whole numbers**
2.1 Simple addition using whole numbers.	2.5 Multiply w/one-digit multipliers.
2.2 Simple addition using whole numbers with renaming.	2.6 Multiply w/one-digit multipliers w/renaming.
	2.7 Divide simple problems.
2.3 Simple subtraction using whole numbers.	2.8 Divide w/remainder (one-digit divisor.).
2.4 Simple subtraction using whole numbers w/renaming.	2.9 Divide with two digit divisor.
	2.10 Compute averages.
2.5 Multiplication w/one-digit multipliers.	2.11 Compute ranges.
2.6 Multiplication w/one-digit multipliers w/renaming.	

(continued)

TABLE 26 Continued

LEVEL 1	LEVEL 2
MATH (continued)	**MATH (continued)**
	3.0 Compute using decimals.
	3.1 Identify order of decimals.
	3.2 Add using decimals.
	3.3 Subtract using decimals.
	3.4 Write percentages as decimals and decimals as percentages.
	3.5 Calculate percentages.
	4.0 Compute using fractions.
	4.1 Match numerical fractions with graphic display.
	4.2 Change improper fractions to mixed numbers.
	5.0 Use weights, measures, measurement scales.
	5.1 Interpret graphs.
	5.2 Read and record measurements.

competencies that were being covered and which competencies were being overlooked. This form was developed for a midterm status report to illustrate the progress of the first class competencies. It became a useful tool for keeping the program on track and for evaluating the achievement level of each group on a weekly basis.

At PET, the competencies grids served as a guide and a communication tool between instructor and program manager. The instructors filled them out weekly, and I collected them to answer questions regarding group progress when asked by managers. These grids also served as a tool for communicating evaluative data to the president of the company.

As an illustration of the importance of a structured communication tool, I (as program manager) neglected to check competency coverage on a weekly basis due to my confidence in the instructors. When the data was provided for the final report, I found that two competencies had been skipped completely because the instructor was working so intently on something else. It is possible that we would have omitted the two competencies and continued with the other instruction if we had been tracking properly. However, I felt quite foolish to find at the end of a program that two of the competencies had been overlooked accidentally.

Pioneer's Chino facility was able to run one ESL class and one BSTQ class simultaneously. However, during peak production times, they requested that the classes be kept to seven participants. Even in doing this, there were times when production emergencies required participants to remain on the line instead of attend class, but this was kept to a minimum. For Pioneer, a 10-week format was selected for the two levels, or 40 hours per level.

In the beginning of the training at the PET Pomona facility, we could run only one session at any given time due to the size and number of rooms available and the production requirements. For the first seven months, the only classes at Pomona were ESL classes due to the large percentage of nonnative speakers. In the eighth month, we started two basic workplace skills classes for a group of supervisors and leads. This group did not require ESL instruction tested out of ESL but still lacked writing skills and some basic math skills.

SUMMARY OF IMPORTANT POINTS

1. Focus on competencies that are required for the achievement of your organization's business goals.

2. A tool for visually tracking competency coverage that can be monitored by the instructors helps keep the training on track.

3. Supervisors need to be trained to support the training with language and behaviors.

4. Two-hour class lengths are effective for BSTQ.

5. A class size of nine to twelve participants is an ideal size.

6. Identify the number of employees that the organization can have off the floor or line at any given time.

7. Divide the competencies or skills into levels which can be covered in approximately 20 to 24 two-hour sessions.

8. If customers request logistical or curriculum changes to the program, advise them of the impact on the total program.

7 | DEVELOP THE CURRICULUM AND MATERIALS

Step 3: Develop the Curriculum and Materials

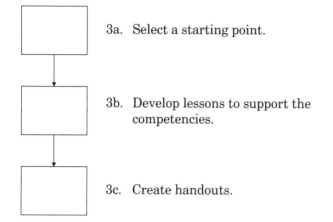

3a. Select a starting point.

3b. Develop lessons to support the competencies.

3c. Create handouts.

Phase II—Development Process

Step 3 consists of the above three parts.

As step 2 of the Development Phase is completed, a set of competencies for each instruction level will have been developed and step 3, Develop the Curriculum and Materials, can begin. This is a critical step because it identifies specific, measurable behavioral objectives that will apply to each of the competencies and lessons that lead to a mastery of those behaviors.

With a customized BSTQ program, some development time is needed before the beginning of training so that the designers or instruction team can develop exercises and worksheets to support the curriculum. The amount of time available will vary from organization to organization. A minimum of five days should be allowed with 10 days being ideal. If more time than this is spent on up-front development, it could result in wasted effort as the program begins to grow and change. This development should focus on materials and exercises for each competency. As these materials are developed, they can be filed according to specific competencies, providing a base of materials from which to draw. Commercially prepared materials, when appropriate ones can be found, can be filed at this time also. The ideal result would be to have two or three customized worksheets with a leader's guide developed for each competency before training begins.

Materials developed this way at the beginning provide the instructor with a strong base. These materials also provide examples of work-related exercises that can be used as models for more development. However, as the materials are used, the instructional team may find that a different format would be more effective with a particular group. For this reason, it would be a waste of time and effort to delay the program while a large quantity of training material is developed. Again, the BSTQ training models the customer focus of total quality by continuing to seek feedback from all program customers (participants, management, and the organization) and adjusting the curriculum as needed to meet customer requirements.

3A. SELECT A STARTING POINT

At this point in the development phase, stacks of workplace forms, process sheets, organization communication, signs, and manuals have been collected. This can be an overwhelming amount of information. A major concern then, is how does one decide where to begin? The following are some tips to keep in mind:

- Begin with an area of instruction where immediate results will be visible. It gets the program off to a good start. (Examples: safety issues, damage reports, clarification of job instructions.)

- Begin with an area of instruction that is important to the participants. This increases enthusiasm. (Examples: Identifying and describing safety issues at work and how safety benefits each employee; calculating accurate times on time cards; using military time where appropriate.)

- Begin with work-related materials that contain something familiar to the participants. This allows them to feel good about what they already know while they are working on skills that need improvement. (Example: Verbally describing tasks they perform as they learn to identify steps in a process.)

- Begin with the lowest level of competencies on the competency chart. If they are too simple for the specific group, move on quickly. Let them feel successful with what they already know.

3B. DEVELOP LESSONS TO SUPPORT THE COMPETENCIES

The next step is to follow these model lessons and structure an exercise for the individual group that will develop these competencies. Several individual competencies, with sample lessons for each competency, are given in Appendix B.

As the designer or instructor develops lessons and materials that teach the identified competencies, and before selecting specific methods and exercises, the instructor should ask the following:

- What do I want the participants to be able to do as a result of this lesson or activity? (Target the competency.)

- Is this the best way to get those results? (Evaluate the effectiveness of the activity.)

- Is this the best use of the participant's time? (Evaluate the effectiveness of the activity.)

- Can the activity be completed in the available time so the lesson will be effective? (Is success with this activity feasible given the available time and facilities?)

- How am I going to know if the participant can perform the behavior? (Plan to evaluate the results of the activity.)

When these questions are answered satisfactorily, the designer can design the lesson and the activities more effectively. Asking these same questions will help to test the appropriateness of the lesson after it is designed.

As the exercises are developed, the designer will notice that the lesson objectives encompass behaviors, measurement methods, and evaluation methods. The competencies and supporting behavioral objectives add structure to the program and are intended to be minimum guidelines. Appendix B describes the process of writing behavioral objectives and provides basic information on training design.

You can use the following steps to develop work-related exercises. As a guide, you may want to use a competency from either the Toro competencies or the PET competencies in Appendix B.

1. Select one of the competencies from the BSTQ competencies.

2. Select work-related materials, information, or situations that you will use to develop the competency.

3. What will the learners be able to do as a result of the exercise to develop the competency?

4. How do you plan to provide for the visual learning needs of the learner?

5. How will you involve the learners so they can learn by doing something with the information?

6. How will you know if the learners have achieved the objective of the exercise?

Use the "Competency-Based Lesson Development" worksheet in Figure 7.1 to summarize and clarify the lesson development.

3C. CREATE HANDOUTS

It is especially important with basic skill learners that written exercises be typed, spelled correctly, and written in clear type, preferably a serif font. These handouts should be planned and not written at the last minute.

Never use all capital letters in material for basic skill learners. Many people learn to read words with the help of the shape of the word. Words that are typed in all capital letters have no distinct shape to them and are more difficult to read.

The following is a list of qualities that make handouts effective:

Competency: _____

Objective:

_____

_____

_____

Exercise Description:

_____

_____

_____

_____

Materials:

_____

_____

_____

_____

Process:

_____

_____

_____

_____

FIGURE 7.1. **Competency-Based Lesson Development.**

- Clear and uncluttered.

- No typos.

- Use graphics for contrast.

- Lots of white space.

- Use upper and lower case letters appropriately.

Lesson Plan Review

If you are the program manager or a new curriculum designer (you might be both), there are a lot of small details to remember in designing instruction sessions and materials. The following questions serve as a guide for points to check as you review your lesson plans for inclusion of major design considerations.

Objectives

- Are the objectives stated in terms of what the participants should be able to do as a result of the training session?

- Have you allowed enough time to achieve the behavioral objectives?

Presentation

- Does your plan cover what you are going to teach and how you are going to teach it?

- How will you get the interest of the participants so they are receptive to the learning?

- Is each topic compartmentalized so there is closure before going on to another topic?

- Have you planned a transition from one topic to another, especially as a bridge between sessions?

- Can you relate each topic to the workplace with an example?

- Has instruction been sequenced so that "easier-to-learn" or "necessary-before-going-on" material is given first?

- How will you verify that learning objectives have been met?

- If using discussion sessions, have you planned key questions to elicit information and guide the discussion?

- Have you added appropriate visual aides where possible?

- Have you listed all required equipment and materials for ease of assembly before the session?

THE TORO COMPANY

The Toro Company had an agreement with their vendor, Crosby Quality Education System, regarding certified trainers and training materials. For this reason, no direct simplification of materials was addressed. Instead, the basic workplace skills curriculum at Toro focused on process skills, basic language skills, math skills, and learning skills.

As discussed earlier, instructors are often the curriculum designers. In the Toro program, the first instructor was strong in developing work-related materials and was also quite adept at using the computer. In one week of up-front development time, he had a good base of materials developed to support the reading and writing competencies. This material required a great amount of written response and was geared to learners of average achievement level and above. He was quite successful with his training groups. His ability to guide learners through material that was a bit difficult was commendable. He was able to keep their motivation high and took the learners beyond their comfort zone on a regular basis. His weakness was in adapting the materials to the needs of lower achievement levels.

As ESL groups began to graduate and enter BSTQ training, a slightly different approach was required. Written work needed to be more basic and there still needed to be much routine oral practice. ESL learners need practice with word order and sentence construction. Fortunately, the instructor who had been doing the ESL training became available to do BSTQ training with these groups. This instructor understood the language skill ability of each of these groups and was able to customize the program for them.

Another special group at Toro consisted of seven slower learners. Some of these individuals had learning disabilities and at least one had special emotional and self-esteem needs. This group required a special treatment of the curriculum including hands-on exercises with objects that could be manipulated for math comprehension, a great deal of repetition on basics, and a lot of encouragement. They progressed as far as possible given their limitations, with a definite improvement in self-esteem. This was a big step for the individual with emotional stability needs and there was great improvement in the ability to participate in work improvement processes. The others began to feel they could learn, allowing them to be more included in the work environment than they were before.

PIONEER ELECTRONICS TECHNOLOGY, INC. (PET)

PET had not selected a specific total quality improvement vendor when the basic workplace skills training began. They followed the Japanese philosophy of Kaizen, and they expected the 5S approach to organizing the workplace to be followed along with several general guidelines for problem solving.

The first two levels of BSTQ concentrated on basic reading, writing, and computation skills. Skills for ISO 9002 certification were approached by describing work processes, discussing process improvement steps, and discussing possible actions to take in order to make these improvements.

A large percentage of the workforce qualified for ESL training, and within that group the needs were also varied. For learners who entered at lower levels of ESL, it became necessary to add some basic sound and phonics work to the curriculum. For the lowest ESL groups, some beginning handwriting instruction was required. Although this skill had not been included in the list of competencies, it was critical to the development of other skills. Even though I was quite experienced at developing BSTQ competencies, I had made the common mistake of assuming that a critical skill existed. I assumed that all adults know how to hold a pencil and make letters. Watching how this group labored at writing the simplest of words and observing that the sentences they wrote on the flip chart appeared quite primitive, similar to the first writing attempts of a youngster in kindergarten or first grade, I recognized that this deficiency was holding them back.

Instead of telling this group they needed to learn to write, I asked if they would like some help with their letters and handwriting. Their response was so enthusiastic that I knew it would be all right to bring in elementary school writing paper with divided lines. The instructor then worked a few minutes at the beginning of every class to show them how to hold a pencil and how to make the letters. These were skills that we had not even considered, but they made a great deal of difference in the rest of this group's work.

Another small class of native English speakers at PET had an unusual mix of employees. One was an advanced ESL learner who had missed the other classes, and others had underdeveloped basic skills for various reasons. I was observing this class one morning when a participant, who stuttered badly when he first entered the class, looked up, smiled broadly, and said, "I'm reading a lot better than I was when I came in. I can tell." He repeated this observation and it seemed that every muscle in his body smiled. This was one of those special happenings that I wish I could share with everyone. There was no statistical documentation for it, but there was no doubt in my mind that the quality of this man's work would be improved forever.

Experiences like this emphasize the importance of approaching each new group of learners with a set of competencies, some developed curriculum material, and a customer focus that makes it possible to adapt additional material to the specific needs of the learners.

The first BSTQ groups at PET's Pomona facility consisted of supervisors, leads, and advanced ESL learners. The curriculum for this group had to be fast paced and focused on basic writing and speaking skills. Their math skills were not as weak as their language skills so the first 10-week session really focused on the language they needed in their jobs. This included some basic work in giving directions and on-the-job training. This group was fun to work with because their abilities were so much greater than their language skills. This meant that they could learn very quickly and the instructor was challenged to stay ahead of them. This group also required the development of materials and exercises that no other groups at that facility would use.

Fortunately, the instructors had a breadth of knowledge in manufacturing, total quality improvement, and ISO 9000 so they could vary the content for each individual group.

A third level of basic workplace skills that was developed for supervisors and leads was based on Kaizen philosophy, 5S, and beginning statistical process control concepts. This content (detailed in Table 25) was another level of BSTQ after BSTQ 1 and 2 and involved some of the specific tasks required in their jobs along with an introduction to basic statistical process control concepts. The instruction team developed the curriculum in collaboration with the production department manager. The curriculum included computing formulas and completing reports that were required from most of the group members. One unexpected and especially rewarding outcome of this training was that during this class, three of the seventeen nonnative speakers of English took the initiative to enroll in night classes to improve their English. Their jobs were changing and the changes required very different skills. These employees had been leaders in the Pioneer workplace for years and were skilled craftsmen who had excellent rapport with the workers. They knew how to direct the tasks and get the most production from the workers. Now their management was requesting them to provide reports, calculate efficiency reports, plan for line balance, involve employees in problem solving, and step into a more proactive role as supervisors. For this, they needed an additional set of skills. The competencies identified in the following table (Table 27) were the focus of an additional training session for supervisors and leads.

TABLE 27 Basic Skills for Total Quality 3: A Course for Supervisors and Leads at Pioneer Electronics Technology, Inc., Pomona, California

Manufacturing

6.0 Apply manufacturing concepts to work-related forms and processes.

6.1 Figure and monitor scrap ratio.

6.2 Demonstrate understanding of cycle time.

6.3 Use standard time.

6.4 Monitor efficiency and demonstrate understanding of how to improve efficiencies.

6.5 Demonstrate knowledge of line balance basics.

    6.5.1 Use a stop watch to record times at work stations.

    6.5.2 List and graph individual station cycle times.

6.6 Demonstrate basic understanding of 5S approach.

    6.6.1 Clearing up.

    6.6.2 Organizing.

    6.6.3 Cleaning.

    6.6.4 Standardizing.

    6.6.5 Training and discipline.

6.7 Name and practice steps in the Plan, Do, Check, Act cycle.

(continued)

TABLE 27 Continued

Reading and Writing

7.0 Writing and communicating daily work procedures.

7.1 Record work processes.

7.2 Communicate work instructions.

7.3 Use company (PET) format for preparing work procedures.

7.4 Demonstrate understanding of PET policy regarding approval and release of documents.

Math (Foundation for Statistical Process Control)

8.0 Use Beginning SPC Skills.

8.1 Compute averages.

8.2 Compute percentages.

8.3 Compute ranges.

8.4 Demonstrate understanding of sampling.

8.5 Gather and display data.

8.6 Begin to read and interpret control charts.

8.7 Demonstrate understanding of SPC vocabulary and concepts.

8.8 Demonstrate knowledge of SPC tools.

SUMMARY OF IMPORTANT POINTS:

1. Allow some development time up front.

2. Do not let the curriculum become rigid; retain flexibility.

3. Vary the materials for different groups.

4. If skills other than those identified in the competencies are required, teach them.

5. If something does not work, change it.

IMPLEMENTATION

COMMUNICATE WITH INTERNAL CUSTOMERS

Step 1: Communicate with Internal Customers

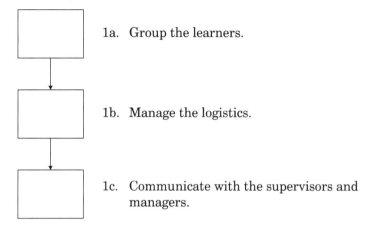

1a. Group the learners.

1b. Manage the logistics.

1c. Communicate with the supervisors and managers.

Phase III—Implementation Process

This phase consists of the following three steps:

Step 1. Communicate with internal customers.

Step 2. Seek continuous feedback and evaluation.

Step 3. Celebrate success.

Phase III, Implementation, begins as the mechanisms are created for moving learners from the work area into the class-room. This is the phase that makes all of the assessing, figuring, talking, listening, and planning a reality. Up until now BSTQ has been only an idea.

The first step, Communicate with Internal Customers, is a process of the following three interrelated activities.

1a. Group the learners.

1b. Manage the logistics.

1c. Communicate with the supervisors and managers.

The next step is to create both the short-term or immediate schedule and the long-range schedule of the complete project. As you begin to develop this long-term picture of the training program, you will create a visual display depicting the length and depth of the BSTQ training program.

1A. GROUP THE LEARNERS

Once you have identified the skill deficiencies of the workforce and you know who needs to be trained, and after the assessment data is entered into a data base and program development is underway, class lists can be created. The most effective criteria for grouping learners in BSTQ includes several different elements. Among them are assessment scores, production requirements, and urgency of skill improvement.

Assessment Scores

The first element to consider is assessment scores because the data is available and easily sorted. This sorted data allows you to assemble a group of learners with similar skills, based on the data. You should be able to tell if the learners have mastered addition and subtraction and begin to fall behind in multiplication, or if they demonstrate adequate skills until they get to division. The learners could be strong in math (as are many ESL learners) and weak in reading and writing. It is also possible that they could be terrible at taking tests and have a lot more skills than indicated, or that they could have copied the answers from another employee. This is not necessarily cheating but a survival tactic to compensate for the lack of skills. Assessment data is only an indication, a place to begin identifying criteria for meeting the needs of the learner.

Production Requirements

The second element to consider is production requirements. Actually, this usually turns out to be the first consideration in the final group assignment. It is beneficial to work with each supervisor ahead of time to identify the maximum number of employees from each line or area that can be in training at a specific time. Encouraging involvement up front is more likely to gain cooperation and commitment and is consistent with the quality principle of customer focus.

This second element is easier to manage if accurate data on employee assignment is contained in the database. Even when this information is present in the database, it often becomes inaccurate by the time it is needed due to frequent reassignment of employees, especially in manufacturing. The problem of inaccurate data can be solved by having personnel or supervisors print out a list of changes in assignments at regular intervals. With this information, it would be possible to maintain an accurate database.

Supervisors need to have class lists in time to cover for those employees in training. In most cases, providing supervisors with class lists a week or two before a new wave of training begins is recommended. If supervisors receive lists too soon, they might not get around to checking them until the last minute. If they receive them a week ahead of time, they seem to deal with them right away. Find the time frame that works best for your customers. If there is going to be a scheduling problem on which you need their special cooperation, approach it one-on-one during the early scheduling stages.

1B. MANAGE THE LOGISTICS

Once you have identified the skill deficiencies of the workforce and have selected the first training groups, the next step is to create the long-range schedule. As you begin to develop this long-term picture of the training program, you will create a visual display depicting the length and depth of the BSTQ training program. This is to demonstrate an understanding of and sensitivity to business concerns and can be used to work in partnership with the organization.

On the other hand, a lack of stability will affect the overall success of the program. What makes your customers happy today may keep you from producing the results they want in the end. For example, requests to cut class size for the purpose of lessening the impact on production will also add to the length and cost of the program. In the end, someone responsible for tracking the costs will ask why there are more classes, and therefore more costs, than were originally planned. When responding to customer requests for changes in this way, you can take the following action:

- Advise them of the impact that honoring their request will have on the program and let them make the decision.

- Recap this change and its predicted impact on the program in writing.

- Provide the right person with the information about the impact on the training budget (this is the person who will have the ultimate responsibility for the budget.)

Finding that balance between maintaining standards and demonstrating flexibility requires some expertise. It is easier to achieve that balance if you keep your primary responsibility in mind while considering the needs of the individual customers. This requires fine-tuned communication skills, problem-solving and conflict management skills, vision, and a positive attitude. Remember that all of the management personnel in the organization are under constant pressure to increase quality while producing product and financial results. Training adds value when it facilitates achievement of quality goals rather than getting in the way.

Schedule Training Rooms

First, training rooms must be scheduled for the extent of the training or at least for the extent of this wave of training. A wave of training consists of all the BSTQ training taking place within the same 10 to 12 weeks. It signifies the beginning of a set number of classes, similar to a semester, quarter, or six-week period in education. It is also helpful to begin all of a particular round of training in the same week, and wait until all of the classes are finished to consider that round completed. Otherwise, keeping track of classes becomes your worst logistical nightmare.

It is fairly simple to figure how many classes can be in session during a round of training. If there are two available rooms, no more than two classes can be in session at any given time. With two available training rooms and two instructors, as many as 24 to 36 employees can be trained at the same hour on the same day. Does this number fit the limitations presented by production or other business concerns? As previously indicated, 7 to 10 percent of the production or service workforce is usually the maximum number of employees who can be in training at the same time without over-straining production requirements.

Each training room must have a writing board on the wall, a flip chart, a supply of chart pads, dry markers, and markers for flip chart use. There should also be an overhead projector in each room, but you can get by without one. The board and the flip chart are essential equipment for the classroom. Figure 8.1 shows a handy checklist that can be used to ensure that all items are covered.

	One classroom of adequate size for each learning group available on a regular basis during training.
	Classroom environments conducive to learning (i.e., low noise level, adequate heat or air conditioning, clean).
	Dedicated flip chart.
	Writing board (on wall).
	Audio visual equipment, overhead projector.
	A table or desk for the instructor.
	Some storage space (i.e., shelves or an extra table).
	Other.

FIGURE 8.1. **Classroom Set-Up Checklist.**

Schedule Instructors

Are instructors available for all of the scheduled classes? This seems too elementary to mention. However, because you may want to use subcontractors as instructors, their availability may affect the schedule. Organizations tend to forget that subcontracting instructors have to plan ahead and therefore may have scheduled other classes if the ones in question have not been confirmed.

Another element to consider is varying shifts. If an instructor is needed for a 6:00 a.m. class, which instructor is available? Also, that person should be assigned the next two classes so their work day is manageable. If you want the best efforts from the best instructors, schedule their classes in sequence so they can manage their work day productively.

If you are using internal trainers, the same considerations apply. Too often, internal people are asked to do training in addition to all of their other responsibilities. They will need time to clear their own participation with their managers and to plan coverage for their own job responsibilities. Training is not as simple as it appears. It requires planning, preparation and a lot of energy. It is more than performing in front of an audience.

Purchase Classroom Supplies
for Each Group

A three-ring binder is useful to have for each participant. Use index tabs to provide order to the notebooks which will be built from loose leaf assignments and notebook paper. The tabs are used also to introduce or reinforce the concepts of indexes and categories. Other helpful equipment for individual use is pencils, extra erasers, and rulers.

Each classroom needs to have the following supplies:

- notebook paper.
- three-hole punch.
- electric pencil sharpener.
- paperback dictionaries (approximately one per person).

As the training program evolves, it is easy to overlook these first-day details in preparation for each new group entering

	One notebook for each learner.
	Notebook paper.
	Dividers with tabs.
	Pencils.
	Chart pads, markers.
	Dry erase markers and board cleaner.
	Individual pencil erasers.
	Three-hole punch.
	Electric pencil sharpener.
	Paperback dictionaries (one per person in class).
	Other.

FIGURE 8.2.   **Start-Up Supplies for the Classroom.**

training. You can use the list in figure 8.2 "Start-Up Supplies" to refer to for the start-up of each new round of training.

Establish a Home Base for Instructors

Is there an area where the external instructors can store materials, receive and deliver messages, and establish a base? These details assist the process of building a partnership between the organization and the instructional team. In addition, these considerations help to ease the day-to-day stress of teaching in one room without much contact with the other areas of the company. The success of any long-term training program is improved if the instructors feel a sense of belonging and acceptance. It is important to avoid isolating the BSTQ training and its instructors from the organization. When they are involved as partners, they are more likely to focus on quality and business goals in the daily instruction.

Notify Participants and Supervisors of Class Assignments and Schedules

After clearing the class lists with the individual supervisors, it is time to notify the participants. There are several acceptable ways to do this including any combination of the following:

- The program manager visits each supervisor's area of responsibility and announces the start of the program and the first participants from that area. At this time the program manager positions the program as part of an organizationwide, ongoing learning process which will prepare employees for participation in the organization's quality initiative.

- The program manager conducts an orientation meeting for supervisors. This could happen at the second or third focus group meeting. It would be helpful if the CEO or general manager could begin this meeting with a statement of support. At this meeting, the program manager briefs the supervisors on the schedule, the participants, and the important points to include in this initial announcement. These points include the ones the program manager has been using to position the program. Behaviors that are supportive of the program versus nonsupportive behaviors should be modeled. A suggested script could be provided.

- Supervisors announce the names of the people who will be participating during this first wave of training. This can work if the orientation meeting described above has been held.

- The program manager goes to the individual participants and explains the program and why they have been selected to participate. This is very time consuming and almost impossible in a large program implementation, but it is very effective.

- Class lists are posted where participants can read them. This will work in combination with one or two of the approaches above or with the last waves of a very long, successful training program.

Manage Participant Resistance

With every new group of participants, there will be some who resent being in this type of training. This resentment usually has to do with their individual perceptions of what the training is about and why they have been selected. There is no training in business that compares to basic skills training when it comes to ego impact. Being identified as lacking in the most basic of functional life skills such as reading, writing, addition, subtraction, and multiplication can communicate to their peer group that they don't "measure up" to the basic requirements for getting along in life. When your basic work skills are not adequate and you know that many changes are occurring in your job, it is very frightening.

People who have built a reputation as informal leaders either by being popular or skilled or tough may resent the risk of having deficiencies discovered. They also may resent being grouped with employees who have been viewed as having less skill. The biggest issue seems to be the chance they will be "found out." These employees typically have little confidence in their classroom learning ability and they don't know how they will be perceived. Others continue to see themselves above the group and neglect to look at their own areas for improvement. They would rather continue to be leaders where they are than to risk moving into a skill level where they might have to stretch. This is one instance where the original assessment can be valuable. The project manager can sit down with the employee and review that person's strengths and weaknesses.

We must remember that the people who will participate in BSTQ training have been getting by some way until now. They usually have sophisticated compensating skills which have helped to hide their skill deficiencies. They also have supportive networks of people who enable them to get by. They have put enormous effort into concealing their lack of skills. When we identify them and make their deficiencies public, they need to know they're OK and they need to know what will happen to them in their peer group, in the workforce, and in the community.

The First Day Jitters

Because each group of learners will be a team, each group will go through the normal stages of growth that a team goes through.

From our team-building sessions, we know the stages to be form-ing, storming, norming, and performing. Each new group then will be in the forming stage. Each learner, or group member will be wondering:

- Why am I here?

- How will I fit in?

- What does being here mean to my other relationships at work?

- What is going to happen to me here?

- Will I look foolish, smart, better than others, worse than others?

- Will I be accepted if I'm not good at this or have weak-nesses that are discovered by the group?

- Will I fail?

It is important on the first day to answer as many of these unspoken questions as possible. The instructor can do this by do-ing the following:

- Define the purpose of the class as it relates to the business goals and personal goals (identify personal goals through discussion.)

- Describe the curriculum.

- Address how they will be evaluated.

- Define classroom standards and expectations.

- Ask how they feel about being here and what they want to learn.

- Have the participants write learning goals for themselves to include a long-term personal goal and a goal for this 10-week session.

These efforts will not necessarily satisfy everyone in the group. Some individuals' concerns will be the results of past classroom experiences, and these will be more difficult to ease.

Fears based on past experiences are often manifested as negative attitudes. Easing these fears can only be done by providing successful experiences.

Program Start-Up Checklist

Another activity that is important on the first day is to verify that the class list and attendance sheet reflect the actual class participants. The first few sessions can be a time of adjusting the class lists to assure the maximum level of success for the participants. I seldom recommend separating participants who do not get along, because this is an opportunity to build relationships. I do, however, sometimes recommend separating participants who are so helpful to each other that one of them will not grow and learn. Firming up class lists is an important beginning session task.

Name cards are helpful for the instructor during these first few sessions. They also lend an official air to the training sessions.

1C. COMMUNICATE WITH THE SUPERVISORS AND MANAGERS

It is now critical to communicate constantly with all of your internal customers on a regular basis. The BSTQ program manager's skills in balancing organizational concerns with requirements for a successful program implementation will be very visible and important. It is at this point that the organization is going to realize that training Sue, John, and Steve means that for two days per week, for two hours, these employees will not be available to do the work they have always done.

Involving supervisors and managers from all areas of the company in the training as supporters, participants, coaches, or any role they want to assume can only benefit the participants, the organization, and the learning that takes place. I have already mentioned informal meetings with individual managers as being helpful. These brief meetings should be routinely conducted on a spontaneous basis and recorded informally. Never assume that a manager doesn't want to be consulted on training topics or invited to observe or participate in class. When organization personnel of any level visit the classroom, it is beneficial to provide them with some guidelines for observation or participation. Because observing lends itself to evaluation, they may tend to evaluate based on classroom models from their past which may or may not have been successful. For this reason, I developed the following guidelines:

- Look for specific skills and knowledge that can be reinforced on the job.

- In conversations with employees, be supportive of the training.

- Provide some practice on the job.

- Notice that an employee is using the skills observed in training and say so.

- Clarify anything you don't understand with the instructor or with the program manager.

- Provide the instructor or the program manager with constructive feedback.

- Continually advise the trainers of any skills you would like to have learned or reinforced.

- If you would like to present a particular skill or exercise to the class, please let us know. We welcome your participation.

It is helpful part way through any BSTQ program to have a brief progress report meeting for the supervisors, managers, and any other personnel who have frequent contact with the participants. These briefings can serve to inform others of current training achievements and reinforcement needs. It may be very difficult to get these meetings scheduled due to the heavy demands on available time. If the critical element of organizational support needs to be developed, then the program manager should be more persistent in scheduling at least one mid-session meeting.

THE TORO COMPANY

The ESL assessment was completed first at Toro since the ESL population was small. The ESL employees who were found to have adequate verbal English skills went on to BSTQ training. This was the first class group to be identified. The other classes were composed of employees with similar scores and therefore similar training needs. These classes of 12 were each formed before the assessment was completed. This was due to the number of employees involved in taking the assessment that required hand scoring. Each supervisor reviewed the class lists and the schedule for possible conflict with production requirements. So the criteria for grouping in this case were ordered as follows:

1. English language proficiency.

2. Assessment scores.

3. Production requirements.

4. Shift assignments.

Participants in the first two waves of training classes at Toro were hand selected by sorting through the assessments. The reason we needed to select the participants by hand for this was the length of time required to score and enter data for this huge number of assessments. Another contributing factor was that it took a long time to get the Toro training tracking software up and running and an employee trained to input data. When this was finally accomplished, it was much easier to select participants using the assessment scores as primary criteria. It was also possible to predict a completion date for the program.

Toro maintained this database and kept it separate from personnel records, as promised. It was strictly used for training information. Two tracks of training began at the same time at Toro; ESL and BSTQ. This required two training rooms and two instructors. Later, this changed to two training rooms of BSTQ in session at one time and finally only one room of BSTQ.

The difficulties with scheduling training rooms for the lengthy training program at Toro were discussed earlier. Each time a new training program begins at Toro, scheduling rooms is one of the challenges. I suspect this is true in most organizations.

The instructors had a small area with a desk and a telephone that they shared. This changed from time to time over the two years that the program was in session, but there was always a homebase of some sort.

In addition, the program manager had a cubicle with a telephone, desk space, and storage space. The program manager used this space for counseling. It could also be used as a place to leave messages for any of the instructors or the program manager.

When the second- and third-shift classes were scheduled, employees were paid overtime to stay late at the end of the third shift or come in early at the beginning of the second shift. One instructor was able to come in at 6:00 a.m. and the other instructor stayed an hour later at the end of the first shift. This way, covering second and third shifts did not create a hardship for either instructor.

One thing that the program at Toro proved again and again was that each new class would have to be treated just as though it were the first class in the training. Participants needed to have a lot of communication with the program manager and the instructor when each new group entered the program. Every time we thought the program could stand on its own without being sold to the new participants, we experienced resistance. With each new wave of training, we had to go to the floor and let individuals know we were looking forward to having them in class. Even with this type of involvement on our part, there were two employees who were assigned to a class but never attended.

This resistance does not appear to be as significant in the groups that enter as ESL learners because these groups of employees know they need English instruction and are quite grateful to have it offered to them at work. Resistance is first noticed in the group of English-fluent ESL learners and in the English-speaking groups. Although this is a generalized statement, I have documented cases of resistance in groups of learners and there are continuously more occurrences in these last two groups. This resistance requires a lot of involvement on the part of the program manager and the instructor and includes individual reassurance and counseling until the learners feel more comfortable in the BSTQ classroom.

At Toro, one of the learners in the group of fluent ESL learners was very angry when we asked her to be in the first round of BSTQ classes. Her comment was, "I wasn't hired here to use my brain. I was hired to assemble sprinklers. If I have to use my brain, I'll go somewhere else."

I answered, "And we know you can. But you know what, you have the opportunity to go to class anyway!"

I never mentioned it to her again, but I walked by her station many times and talked about other things. Finally, before the last round of classes, I walked up to her and invited her to attend the class. Last chance. If she didn't like it she could leave. She attended and she stayed, and she did very well. Voluntarily.

PIONEER ELECTRONICS TECHNOLOGY, INC. (PET)

At Pioneer Electronic Technology's Chino plant, the first classes to be scheduled were six ESL classes that were grouped by language ability, six BSTQ classes comprised of fluent ESL learners, and native speakers of English who needed remediation of math and language skills. One class of ESL and one of BSTQ were in session continuously.

At the PET Pomona facility, the training began with the six lowest levels of ESL in six classes that each met twice per week. One classroom, three sessions, every day, four days per week. However, six months into implementation the participants still were not using English outside of the classroom. (This was an important evaluation point for the president of PET.) So the instructional team, consisting of the personnel manager, the BSTQ instructor, the manager of manufacturing operations, and myself, decided to train the supervisors and leads as the first group in BSTQ, so they could support the ESL training by speaking English to employees. Although most of this group of supervisors and leads tested out of ESL, they were bilingual and still resorted to speaking Spanish when giving work instructions. These two classes of supervisors and leads were the first BSTQ classes to begin at Pioneer.

What I learned from this was to begin ESL training with levels that could begin using English the fastest. They would then be able to speak English sooner and they would be able to practice with the less fluent speakers. This was a completely opposite approach from the one the program management team took in the beginning, when we scheduled the people who required the greatest number of hours into training first. We meant well, but there needed to be a middle ground which allowed some of the employees with the least English fluency skills and some of the more fluent people to start at the same time. This would have created a better environment for practicing the new language skills.

At Pioneer, we had almost no problems with learners resenting their involvement in the training program except in one group of native English speakers and in another group of very fluent nonnative English speakers. Having a program manager who can observe and counsel resentful participants is extremely helpful. For example, during the assessment, one employee showed a great deal of resentment. He was a native speaker of English, had been employed for several years at this facility, and had a certain following. He was a large young man who moved with a swagger and maintained an aura of mystery about his personal life.

I cautioned the instructor before the first class that I felt he resented being in class and might be a challenge for her. I offered my support in the form of class observation and counseling. I can not remember the exact moment that his attitude changed, but it was early in the program after realizing he was going to be OK in the class and he was going to learn. The instructor had a way of communicating her genuine caring for the participants and an ability to laugh at her own mistakes. This communicated to the participants that it was a safe place to make mistakes. She began noticing and commenting on his strengths, as she did with everyone. I supported her in this and he found himself getting positive reinforcement for some of his real abilities rather than his attitude.

During a math class, he came up to her and whispered, "I don't know how to do division. When I was in school, the teacher laughed at me in front of the room when I wrote the problems on the board, so I quit trying." The instructor's response was, "It's OK if you don't know division because we're going to spend time on it. Remember, we don't laugh at mistakes in here, unless they're mine. We learn from them." He learned to do division, and mastered all of the math competencies. He also started writing poetry again because being in the class reminded him he could write, and he came in often during lunch to talk with us. He stopped in recently and made the comment, "If I had had teachers like her, I might have learned more in school. I have been so motivated by this class that I worked on my writing during Christmas vacation." When the class was over he wrote the instructor a note that said, "I am no longer that scared third grader."

There were other stories in that group. There was one older employee who could hardly write or spell and, at the beginning, would not try. By the end of the sessions he was asking when there would be more classes.

SUMMARY OF IMPORTANT POINTS

1. Schedule training rooms in advance.

2. Confirm class times with instructors.

3. Collaborate with supervisors for scheduling participants.

4. Collaborate with supervisors to communicate class assignments to participants.

5. Provide stability through consistency in class times, days, and rooms.

6. Make changes to the schedule the rare exception.

7. Establish a home base for instructors.

8. Regular audit of environmental details, aided by a checklist, helps maintain program quality.

SEEK CONTINUOUS FEEDBACK AND EVALUATION

Step 2: Seek Continuous Feedback and Evaluation

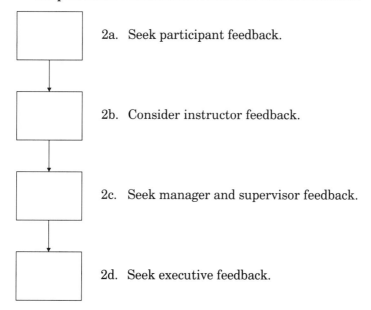

2a. Seek participant feedback.

2b. Consider instructor feedback.

2c. Seek manager and supervisor feedback.

2d. Seek executive feedback.

Phase III—Implementation Process

Step 2 of the Implementation Phase, Seek Continuous Feedback and Evaluation, consists of the above four interrelated activities that embody the customer feedback emphasis of total quality improvement efforts.

The approach used to evaluate BSTQ is based on meeting the requirements of the customer. The critical role of the program manager in BSTQ is to manage the process of identifying and meeting these customer requirements. The program manager manages the communication flow that provides constant feedback to the BSTQ instructional team. This allows the team to communicate with all internal customers of the training program on a regular basis. Evaluation is done weekly with almost constant communication, allowing BSTQ to make adjustments before problems occur. This way, class instructional time can be of maximum benefit to everyone. In today's lean business environments, time spent in training must be optimized to add value for the business.

BSTQ program development, implementation, and evaluation model the customer/supplier relationships of total quality management where feedback and evaluation take place in a constant, flowing manner. It is not something that happens only at the end of a round of training nor only at specific points in the program. It is not an event. It is a constant process of seeking and listening to daily feedback. This contrasts with the classic, widely used Kirkpatrick evaluation method described here, in which assessment pretraining data and post-training data are evaluated at any of four levels:

Level 1:   Participant evaluation.

Level 2:   Content mastery.

Level 3:   Behavioral changes.

Level 4:   Impact on business goals.

The two approaches, the Kirkpatrick model and the BSTQ improvement model, are not mutually exclusive. In fact they can be used together, contributing to the success of the BSTQ training program. However, the Kirkpatrick model alone does not provide feedback on a just-in-time basis as the BSTQ program requires.

2A. SEEK PARTICIPANT FEEDBACK

This level of evaluation is important in BSTQ training. The major reason is that the participants are just beginning their corporate training experience. A positive reaction to training means they are overcoming possible negative classroom experiences of the past.

In the BSTQ program, this feedback should be happening on a continuous basis as the program progresses. The ending evaluation is important but should not take the place of constant feedback from the participants as the program progresses. Constant feedback from the participants can be supported by and built into the program in the following ways:

- Training can be positioned as learner-driven in the beginning. "The company is dedicated to achieving total quality (or other appropriate business goals). This training is for you because you will be an important part of that achievement. Let us know if you want to learn something specific. Let us know if we need to change something about the classes."

- Constant instructor encouragement of feedback. "Thank you for telling us."

- Meetings between individual participants and program manager. "Your feedback is important."

Openness to feedback and suggestions for ways to improve is a very basic element of the total quality improvement culture. Modeling it here, making it safe for employees to speak up even when their communication skills are unsophisticated, establishes a supportive communication climate. Encouraging differences of opinion in the BSTQ setting introduces the skills for conducting a constant dialogue regarding conflict and problem issues.

It is imperative that the training sessions be a safe place for participants, and it is the instruction teams' responsibility to ensure that safety. Any information or concern that surfaces during the training sessions should be provided to management only if it can be anonymous and relatively generic to ensure anonymity.

At one point, when Toro was beginning to downsize, the ESL class was very concerned. They had heard only rumors, so they feared they might be part of the cutbacks. The instructor helped them do some problem solving so they could see that, even if the rumors were true, they had some options. This allowed them to be less stressed until the communication about the downsizing was clearer.

At the end of many training programs, participant evaluation is conducted by using rating scales for different statements. A similar type of rating scale does not work well with most BSTQ groups. Participants may have little experience with evaluations and their responses tend to be all positive or all average with no real information regarding what worked and what did not work.

At the end of each 10 to 12 weeks of training, instead of using a rating scale the BSTQ instructor will ask the participants to describe in writing how they will use what they have learned on the job and how they intend to keep learning. This activity brings closure to the session and requests some level of commitment from the participant to continue learning. Again, we operate from the premise that there must be something in this training for the participant. Identifying this on an individual basis is important. These comments can be shared with the learning group or with the total graduating group. This process identifies what the participants learned while it is still fresh in their memory, and they are less likely to forget the value of the training.

2B. CONSIDER INSTRUCTOR FEEDBACK

Participant achievement level for each competency can be evaluated every day in the classroom by the instructor. The instructor evaluates the daily achievement by observing individual learners, providing each one with the assistance and encouragement they need. Keeping the number of participants to 15 or less is key to providing this level of evaluation. If a group of learners can not master all of the competencies in a particular area, it is best to focus on the really critical competencies that create a foundation for learning the others.

Track the Progress of Competencies

An effective way to keep track of the progress of competencies for each learning group has been the competency grid mentioned earlier. As lesson plans for the week are written, squares on the grid that correspond with the appropriate competencies can be colored in. This gives the instructor and the program manager a quick visual check of the progress they are making on the competencies. This quick visual identification of areas that are and are not being covered allows a course correction while there is still time. The instructor is also able to keep track of individual achievement on each competency as determined by daily observations, quizzes, and instructor/learner interactions.

The program manager collects or checks the grids each week as a way to remind the instructors to keep them up to date. Filling them in at the end of a 40-hour class is time consuming and

Basic Skills for Total Quality Training

Name: _____ Date: _____

1. What did you like best in the training?

2. How could the training be better for you?

3. What did you learn that you will use most on the job?

4. How can you keep learning after the training ends?

FIGURE 9.1. **Participant Evaluation.**

then becomes an exercise in paperwork. The intent of the grids is to provide a running account of where we are in covering our goals as indicated by the competencies selected for each class. This assures that if a competency is not covered, and therefore, a goal is not reached, we know exactly why.

As the competency grids are discussed by the program manager and instructor, discussion of individual achievement levels, issues, and possible solutions are also discussed. With this collaborative approach, the program manager and instructor can often determine additional methods of working with particular individuals.

An evaluation report to management covering each wave of training can easily communicate coverage of competencies when they have been recorded regularly on a grid. Learner achievement rates on each of the competencies can be presented using a simple bar graph showing the number of learners who mastered 100 percent, 90 percent, and 80 percent of the presented competencies as determined by the instructor. Any additional comments and recommendations can be presented in this report. This can be an effective manner of communicating progress on requirements for program success.

The report, which chronicles the highlights of each particular round of training, records verbal suggestions and anecdotes from participants and managers that indicate the application of skills to the workplace. It also identifies the specific elements in the organization that will influence the results of the program and recommends actions that can be taken to maximize the benefits of the organization's training investment. This report is also an effective means of publicizing supportive gestures. Because the report is distributed to all concerned management personnel, it can highlight effectively the continued importance of their continuing involvement in reinforcing the learning. This publication of recommendations seems to increase the likelihood that important issues will be acted upon.

2C. SEEK MANAGER AND SUPERVISOR FEEDBACK

Managers and supervisors are closest to the training and the results. Comments, anecdotes, and adjustments to the curriculum, therefore, should flow easily between managers, supervisors, program managers, and instructors. One of the things I have learned about working with management groups is to never take anything for granted. For instance, there may be constant verbal communication that indicates training is meeting supervisory expectations, but when a final evaluation is written, it is difficult to recoup all of those positive comments. The tendency is to focus on the original expectations, clarified or not, and to forget all of the other daily successes and responses to requests for changes.

The program manager can manage this part of the evaluation by documenting feedback from all internal customers on a regular basis, including requests for changes and their impact on the overall training goals. If the program manager recaps ongoing training successes and anecdotes in the form of brief memos to management personnel, these memos can serve as a way to record verbal comments on a timely basis. This makes the positive impressions of the training easier to recall for the final evaluation.

The behaviors that the manager or supervisor want to see increased or decreased as a result of the training were identified in the original focus groups of the discovery phase. These behaviors demonstrate the achievement of skills and competencies and can be measured because they can be seen or heard. They should be kept in mind when you gather anecdotes and when you have informal conversations with the managers and supervisors.

In one recent BSTQ class, it was apparent that the participants would not achieve the level of mastery in math of the previous group (although each group made strong individual growth), but their progress in writing processes was excellent. When they entered the class they could not define or describe a process but now they were able to describe sequential steps in a familiar process such as using an ATM or pumping gas. They were still working on describing the steps in their job process.

Writing process steps was an important focus for the total quality manager and the supervisors in the midst of writing job instructions for ISO 9000. When I reported to the supervisors on the progress of this group, I took the process steps the participants had written and posted them on chart sheets around the room. The supervisors and the total quality manager were impressed at the progress the participants had made in writing processes. By staying aware of the group's progress, the supervisors and managers can reinforce behavioral changes indicating improved skills as soon as they see them, and this will help to achieve the organization's goals.

Changes in behavior that allow learners to demonstrate skills will not take place unless the behavior is rewarded on the floor. For example, if trainees are encouraged to spot defects and report them, the person to whom they report needs to have an appropriate response. There have been times when trainees tried this new behavior and the other person involved felt challenged and responded defensively. As the BSTQ trainees begin to try out new skills, other members of the organization will need to learn new skills in response. If the trainees are encouraged to ask questions when they do not understand, the person being asked needs to react in a nondefensive manner.

It requires a skillful program manager to be able to spot the deficiencies in the organizational support system and be able to impact this system positively. There are often several reasons for the nonapplication of learned skills in the workplace that the program manager needs to stay aware of. Some of the reasons may lie in the organizational support system itself. Also, the timing between the actual training results and the implementation of supportive systems sometimes does not coordinate properly. With the BSTQ program manager managing this support system for behavioral change, the organization can experience a better return on its training investment.

If feedback from supervisors and managers indicates that desirable behaviors are not increasing, investigate the opposing forces in the organizational system and launch a multifaceted intervention to allow goals to be accomplished. An example of this successful strategy is described in the Pioneer case study at the end of this chapter.

Examples of some barriers to BSTQ success in the organizational system are listed in Table 28 along with some of the aids to BSTQ success.

2D. SEEK EXECUTIVE FEEDBACK

Executives in the organization need to see a return on their investment of training dollars through program evaluation. They

TABLE 28 Barriers and Aids to BSTQ Success

Goal: Improved Basic Skills for Total Quality and involvement of employees in total quality and continuous improvement efforts, using their skills in problem solving, calculating, questioning, speaking, and communicating.

Barriers	Aids
Lots of overtime, physical exhaustion.	Interactive classes with much participation and content that is relevant to learners.
Heavy production requirements make class attendance difficult.	Attendance is encouraged and temporaries hired to ease production requirements.
Nonsupportive supervisor behaviors.	Educate supervisors regarding supportive behaviors. Supervisors must be committed to training for frontline employees and sold on benefits to work group.
Management talks above employees.	Firm commitment of resources. Executives must value training and support it. Executives make efforts to talk with employees more often.
Other employees put down learners. Organization works to maintain status quo.	Participants must demonstrate skill growth in class and apply it to the workplace. Self-confidence grows. TQM involvement rewarded in the workplace.
Managers expect participants to have no skill deficiencies when they leave class and do not see their role in reinforcement and application.	Educate managers and supervisors as to their role in developing the employees.

need to see the results that they, as individuals, expected to achieve, as well as any other results the program produces. It is the program manager's job to uncover these expectations during the beginning interviews and keep them in mind at all times. Observations of results can be documented and communicated to the executives in a timely manner.

A major difficulty of evaluation lies in trying to link directly positive business results and training. Experts say that it is not necessary to prove that training effects business results, but only to show evidence that there is a connection between them.[3] There are usually some existing data that can be used for this part of an evaluation.

While data can be found to indicate training has a positive impact on business results, it is more important that the executive and the managers of the company connect this data on training to positive business results. Executives may make this connection in different ways. Some will identify specific measurable results such as the following:

- An increase in written suggestions.

- A reduction in inventory errors.

- An increase in defect identification.

- An increase in accurate descriptions of damage.

- An increased ability to describe the work process.

- A reduction in rejects.

- A reduction in rework.

Others may determine that training is one of several elements contributing to the successful achievement of business goals. One of the best indicators of the perceived value of training by the chief executive is the clear commitment of resources to further training. No executive will knowingly allocate funds to useless projects.

The two BSTQ programs in the case studies were implemented due to business requirements. Therefore, this focus drove the training and the curriculum.

THE TORO COMPANY

At Toro, the general manager was an enthusiastic supporter of the training. He spoke briefly at each graduation celebration of

---

3. Geber, Beverly. *Does Your Training Make a Difference?* **Training Magazine.** Lakewood Publications, Minneapolis, MN: March, 1995, pp. 27–34.

the value of continuous learning. He and his directors placed high value on improved self-confidence, individual participant involvement and attitude, improved communication in the workplace, and team problem solving. These were definite improvements in employee skills that the quality initiative would require if it was to be successful.

Participant Evaluation

At each graduation celebration, which was attended by most directors, managers, and supervisors, the general manager was the introductory speaker. Participants were invited to speak in front of the group and describe what the training had meant to them. These were often stories of past struggles and current successes. One man in his thirties was particularly proud of his certificate and he told the group this was the first one he had ever received. These comments caused more than one wet eye among the task-oriented managers.

Each class identified what they would use from their learning and how they could continue learning. Post-training assessment scores (obtained from administering the same instrument that was used for the preassessment) indicated a 17% increase in reading and writing and a 15% increase in math in a 12-week period (see figure 9.2.)

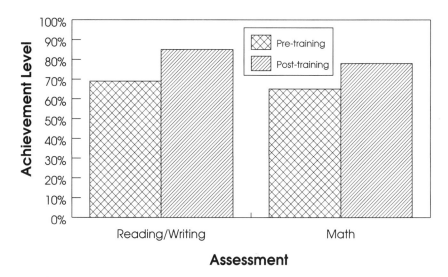

FIGURE 9.2. **Toro BSTQ Competency Achievement, Group 1.**

Today, many of the original participants are active in the total quality activities at Toro. At least three of them are now team leaders and some of them have done some group training themselves. These are good examples that some of the long-term goals for the basic workplace skills training at Toro were achieved.

There were many anecdotes about behavioral changes and their results that were not quantified. There were stories about employees doing the following:

- Being able to describe symptoms of a child during a visit to the emergency room.

- Being able to help their children with math homework.

- Giving clear directions to a visitor in the work area.

- Describing problems on the line.

- Describing the task they were performing for touring customers.

- Taking on tasks of speaking or leading that they were hesitant to take on before the training.

The first classes to go through training requested additional instruction, so a home study course was developed for them. The instructor designed work packets that the graduates could check out, complete, and return for feedback. Out of 12 participants, six signed up for this program and worked through it, four others enrolled in adult education programs, and two went no further at that time.

In addition, the program manager fed anecdotes back to management whenever possible about individual successes as a result of the training. This constant effort to keep program successes visible improved the level of management confidence in the value of the training.

Although I did not numerically or statistically evaluate the BSTQ program at Toro against business results, their business goals were the focus of the training at all times. Lyle Elliott, human resources director for Toro Irrigation Division, was quoted in a September 1994 issue of Workforce Training News regarding the BSTQ training of '91 and '92 and the team training of '93 and '94 as saying, "The investment has paid off. We've had tremendous increases in quality. Over the past two or three years, our submitted quality level (measure of rejects) has dropped threefold, or about 50 percent, and our scrap and re-work has dropped about 60 percent."

Another basic skills assessment was conducted in December 1994, and another round of BSTQ classes began in January 1995. As of this writing, 180 employees have been enrolled in BSTQ classes during this implementation at Toro.

PIONEER ELECTRONICS TECHNOLOGY, INC. (PET)

Pioneer has taken several important steps toward the long-term goal of a better educated workforce by achieving the more imme-diate goals of improved English communication skills and ISO 9002 certification. In the pursuit of those two major goals, many smaller goals were also met.

Small graduation ceremonies were conducted as each class finished BSTQ. These were informal times where cake was served and participants talked about plans for continuing their education. Before serving the cake, the instructor had the gradu-ates write the answers to these two questions, "How are you go-ing to use what you have learned?", and "How can you continue learning?"

During the life of the program (over two and a half years), fewer than five participants dropped out of BSTQ classes. Two of these were long-time employees who had never been in a class-room and began to get very uncomfortable as the learning tasks became more complex.

Each class was evaluated by the instructor as instruction on competencies took place. Evaluation methods included observa-tions, daily work, and frequent quizzes. Final results showed that over 80 percent of the learners achieved over 80 percent of the competencies. This was the original measurement goal iden-tified by management, and the final data show that we exceeded these expectations.

The president of PET had been supportive of the BSTQ pro-gram by dedicating resources and supporting the continuation of classes from the very beginning. He personally wanted to see the increased usage of English. Even after the completion of the English-as-a-Second-Language training, the basic workplace skills program (which included written language and math) would be partially evaluated on the verbal usage of English in the workplace.

Yet, the bilingual supervisors and staff continued to speak Spanish as they had done for years, and the newsletter continued to be translated in Spanish more than one year into the program. As the program came closer to completion, several different approaches to facilitating this transition were attempted. Somehow, the company had to create a necessity for speaking English. This was a clear case of a company trying to make a change in the culture and encountering the organization's attempts to maintain status quo.

Both verbal and written requests from the president's office that English be used as much as possible had little effect. In search of a tangible reason for learners to practice their new skills, the idea of giving them points for speaking English was devised. These points could be accumulated and redeemed for something of perceived value. We asked the learners if there was something they would like the opportunity to earn. They indicated that Spanish/English dictionaries would be their first choice. A Spanish/English dictionary for the classroom was requested earlier because we were using all-English dictionaries. Other suggestions included English and math workbooks and multiplication flash cards. These tangible rewards would assist with the learning process.

The workers began to have some success with speaking English and they gradually overcame their shyness and fear of looking foolish. Their favorite item, the one they all wanted first, was an English/Spanish dictionary. Their next favorite item was multiplication flash cards. At Chino, all of the participants with the lowest English skills earned at least one dictionary, some earned two dictionaries, and several earned more than one reward. Their supervisors were especially supportive and encouraged their English usage. English was also more of a necessity at Chino because the supervisors primarily spoke English. At Pomona, where most of the supervisors were bilingual, the lowest skilled speakers improved and many of them earned dictionaries. In the next level of language proficiency, all of the participants (about 60) earned at least a dictionary and some earned more than one reward.

Work with the Organization to Achieve Results

While the rewards were being earned in the classroom, I was searching for other opportunities to remove barriers to the president's perceived success of the training. His goal of 80 percent competency achievement were being met, and I was still looking for ways to increase the speaking of English.

A missing piece to the puzzle of how to increase the use of English at Pioneer was the realization that English-speaking employees needed to develop skills for encouraging the non-native English speakers. Working with the English-speaking personnel was a key element. As stated earlier, memos requesting the ESL learners to speak English had not caused a lot of change. It was evident that the following points needed to be clarified:

- Expectations of the level of English usage that would be acquired through the instruction of the ESL group must be clarified.

- Behavior that would support new English skills needed to be modeled.

- The English-speaking personnel needed to hear the ESL learners describe specific behaviors that would be helpful.

We decided that possibly the native English speakers and bilingual speakers simply did not know what those supportive behaviors were. The solution was to schedule a meeting with all of the English-speaking personnel with whom employees interacted on a daily basis. At this meeting, the BSTQ instructor modeled the following:

- The rate of delivery (how fast to talk.)

- A way to find out if the new English speaker understands what the fluent English speaker is orally communicating.

- The level of vocabulary usage for the new English speaker.

The instructor also distributed a handout containing some of the work phrases with which the students were working. Two

ESL learners were asked to demonstrate what they needed from the other employees to use their English.

These two new English speakers were specific in requesting that supervisors talk with them in English and write memos in English. These requests were contrary to the general perception of the nonnative-English-speaking workforce. These new English speakers essentially said that they did not want everything translated for them, they wanted a chance to practice speaking English, and they wanted others to be patient when working with them.

These comments were surprising to many of the bilingual employees who really enjoyed building a certain rapport with the workers by sharing the Spanish language. One of the managers related feelings of loss when one of the new English speakers asked her to please talk to him in English. She became aware that perhaps she, as a bilingual employee, used Spanish because she enjoyed it. She used this story to point out to her peer group that they might need to give up some of the social benefits of speaking Spanish to these employees. After this very brief meeting, the bilingual staff became very cognizant of encouraging other employees to speak English. The English-speaking employees expressed appreciation for the insight and the examples of how to work with the new English speakers. This is another example of how people will try to do what is expected of them if they know exactly what the behaviors are and how they're being exhibited. The main points brought out at this meeting were the following:

- English-speaking employees need to encourage nonnative English speakers to be comfortable trying to speak English.

- Nonnative English speakers want to practice but do not want to look foolish.

- Expecting employees to speak English creates a necessity and helps them to learn.

- Speaking a language other than English with employees keeps the nonnative speaker from practicing and learning English. It may improve your Spanish, or Chinese, or other foreign language but it does nothing to improve the other person's English.

This meeting helped highlight the necessity to speak English with employees and also some of the difficulties. Continuing the effort to encourage these new learners would now be up to the company.

SUMMARY OF IMPORTANT POINTS

1. BSTQ encourages constant two-way communication between learners, supervisors, management, instructors, and the program manager. This allows constant evaluation and adjustment in attempting to meet customer requirements.

2. Reporting structures help keep the instruction focused on identified goals.

3. The program manager keeps the program focused on long-term organizational goals and executive expectations.

4. Each organizational group that interacts with the learners needs to know how to support the BSTQ training.

5. Anecdotes that indicate qualitative data about BSTQ can be recorded immediately for best retention.

CELEBRATE SUCCESS

Step 3: Celebrate Success

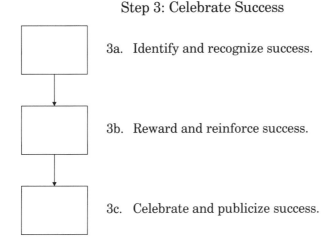

3a. Identify and recognize success.

3b. Reward and reinforce success.

3c. Celebrate and publicize success.

Phase III—Implementation Process

Step 3 of Phase III, Implementation, consists of the above specific groups of behaviors.

Most success stories are reports of individual experiences. These stories are always well received by the organization and by the community. I believe that a training program that proves its success in numbers only, with no concern for the human success stories, may be statistically successful but fail to add lasting value to the organization's TQM effort. When the statistics highlight the success of human beings, making that success more believable, understandable, and reproducible, then the numbers are valuable.

There are other signs of success that we can also take note of in this type of training program.

3A. IDENTIFY AND RECOGNIZE SUCCESS

Attendance and Completion

Attendance itself is a sign of success in this program. Because the program is not mandatory, participants can choose not to attend or later to drop out. In any adult basic skills education program, retaining participants can be an issue. A study by the Comprehensive Adult Student Assessment System (CASAS) in 1989 showed that in a population of 41,317 adult students, 39 percent left school. Of the 39 percent who left, 30 percent left because they attained their goal, which in most cases, was a job or higher education. The Riverside Adult School in Riverside, California indicated that initial enrollment was usually high but the number of students retained until the completion of a course was considerably less. In a presentation to the American Society of Training and Development (ASTD) in May 1994, a review of a partnership project between Northwest Iowa Community College and Coilcraft, Inc. cited drop-out rates of 34 percent in one level of training and 22 percent in the next level.

These programs are representative of typical adult basic education courses and are not the same as BSTQ, although the latter study represents workplace basic skills. However, there are the following similarities:

1. The population is similar in educational background.

2. The level of academic achievement is similar.

3. Self-esteem development needs are similar.

4. The level of work experience is similar.

5. Attendance is voluntary in both programs.

Some differences include:

1. Adult basic education (ABE) usually takes place during personal time or requires a minimum number of participants, which may create a burden for production.

2. BSTQ takes place on company time in most cases.

3. An organization's introduction of BSTQ communicates its importance in preparing the employees to participate in additional total quality training.

At first glance, the retention of participants in these classes is an indication of success. An exodus of large numbers of participants from the program would indicate a problem. In fact, every withdrawal from the program should be investigated for signs that the training is not meeting customer requirements.

Requests for Additional Classes

The many requests that the case study organizations have had for more classes is another indication of success. As each class finished, the participants were asked to identify things they could do to keep learning. Many of them asked for more classes. Long after their classes had finished, several of them asked when more classes were scheduled. The participants always expressed their gratitude to the organizations for providing them with the training.

Application of Skills to Personal Life

There were many stories of the application of skills to personal work life at both study sites. Although the curriculum was work based, we know that when skills are applied in other situations, especially in personal situations, there is more likelihood that the skills will be retained. This is because the skills are seen as personally valuable to the employee. For this reason, the skills are more apt to be integrated with other employee skills, allowing for their retention and recall for other situations.

Seeking Further Education

Another sign of success is when any of the participants seek more education. This is an indication that their self-confidence and their thirst for knowledge has increased. Since one goal of BSTQ is to increase learning skills, participant enrollment in community education or college extension courses is certainly an indicator of success.

3B. REWARD AND REINFORCE SUCCESS

The attitude of the organization toward BSTQ training will effect the success of the training. From the discovery phase through the development and implementation phase, the organization needs to make sure it is reinforcing and rewarding the desired behaviors. If participants are learning to speak up and problem solve, then it is important to notice when they are demonstrating these behaviors in the workplace. When employees express concerns about why they are in class, assure them it is because they are valued by the organization.

When team leaders, supervisors, or managers visit the BSTQ class, they can note exactly what skills are being taught and reinforce those skills when they interact with the participants in the work setting. If the leaders can not visit the training sessions, they can ask the participants what they are learning, whether it is useful, and how they can practice the skill at work.

3C. CELEBRATE AND PUBLICIZE SUCCESS

Any opportunity for celebrating the training and publicizing the results within the organization should be utilized. Obvious opportunities include bulletin boards, newsletters, snapshots, videos, and certificates of completion. Graduation ceremonies lend a note of celebration and closure to any training program. The success of an organization's graduation ceremonies is dependent to a great extent on the cultural background of the recipients. In some cultural groups the individuals do not want to be singled out as having done something special on their own. The program manager needs to be sensitive to these cultural issues when planning organizational celebrations.

A simple graduation ceremony with refreshments served afterward and a few brief congratulatory speeches is one way for the organization to communicate their pride in the learning process and in the people who participate in it.

Tell the Community

The current business climate is very appreciative of companies that make the effort to develop basic work skills in employees. Communities understand that improving the work skills of employees will help keep the unemployment applications down and also contribute to solutions for social problems. Therefore, speaking publicly about such a program is a way to build goodwill for your company. BSTQ training is also an issue facing many organizations today, and therefore companies want to hear about programs that have been successfully implemented by others.

Assigning resources to the development of employees is something every company can be proud of, and it provides an opportunity for excellent public relations articles. Be sure to take

your message to the community by way of presentations to professional organizations, press releases, and even public cable if
appropriate.

When presenting your story to the public, you should avoid
criticizing the quality of public education. That is an issue that
cannot be solved in one presentation, and it will divert attention
from your true message. Your message should consist of a much
more positive, problem-solving approach rather than encouraging comments that place blame on any institution or group of
people.

THE TORO COMPANY

In the Riverside, California area, Lyle Elliott, director of human
resources at Toro, has become a recognized community leader in
the area of literacy. He speaks often at local functions and has
chaired the United Way General Literacy Network for the Inland
Empire of San Bernardino and Riverside Counties. In addition,
Lyle and I have presented collaboratively the Toro case study to
numerous local conferences.

In 1994, after the completion of the first BSTQ training, we
returned to Toro and once again assembled the employees for an
assessment to prepare for a new round of classes. We received a
warm and enthusiastic reception from both the participants and
the team leaders which was in contrast to the fearfulness that
accompanied the assessment in 1990. This time there were few
apprehensive faces although there were some disclaimers about
how much they retained. It was encouraging to see the willingness of the previous participants to participate in this new round
of assessment and classes. These participants were also pleased
to see one of the same instructors that had been involved in the
1990 to 1992 classes return.

Some of this group had not been in a class of any kind for
more than two years, and their assessment scores were low.
Some of the group being assessed this second time had not been
in the earlier BSTQ implementation. The achievement level on
this round of written pretraining assessment was low, but the
gain in the achievement level on the post-training assessment
was greater than it had been in the original training (see figure
10.1.) These new groups of learners made large incremental im-

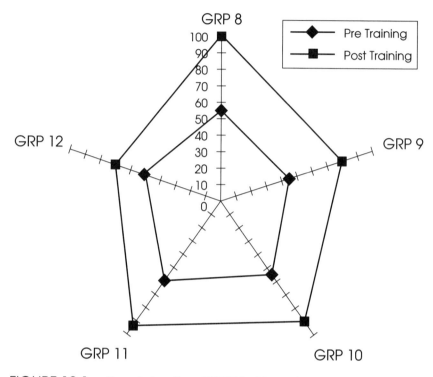

FIGURE 10.1. **Toro Irrigation BWSTQ, Math Session 2, 1995.**

provements in the 10 weeks they were in class. These most recent training groups were not grouped in ability levels, but were assigned by team leaders. Each class consisted of several levels of ability similar to the work groups on the manufacturing floor.

PIONEER ELECTRONICS TECHNOLOGY, INC. (PET)

At Pioneer, where lines operate 10 hours per day, four days a week, two employees from the native-English-speaking class signed up for adult school and one nonnative English speaker from the Chino facility enrolled in adult classes. On a recent visit to the Chino facility I walked through the cafeteria area at lunch time and spoke to several of the program participants. One of the first participants told me he had enrolled in the local community college for the next quarter.

From the Pomona facility, two leads enrolled in English classes and attended them every night until production demands prevented their attending. In the first classes that began as low-level ESL groups, several employees enrolled in community classes. This was perhaps the greatest success of all, because these individuals began with fewer basic skills than any other participants in the Pomona program.

One of the production managers at PET collaborated with us on the curriculum for supervisors and kept the communication about employee classes open and current. He told us often that he wanted these employees to be able to walk into his office and ask him questions anytime they wanted to. He was disappointed when late into the training none of the employees had come to him with questions. They did not seek him out. The instructor encouraged the participants to do this, but nothing happened. Then one day the instructor asked one of the groups if they knew where the production manager's office was located. They informed her they did not know. So the instruction team determined that a field trip to the operations management office was in order. We were not quick in making this happen, but when we did, the results were dynamic.

Each class visited the manager in one group. Their preparatory instructions were to of think of a question they wanted to ask. These sessions were successful with each member of the group participating in the question and answer session. The manager was pleased that they had come to his office. However, he was quite amazed at the things these employees did not know about the company. In addition to the location of this manager's office, these employees wanted to know:

- What his position was.
- What his manager's position was.
- How their bonuses were determined.
- How they were impacted by change in company business results.

English-speaking managers often have no idea of just how isolated the nonnative English speakers are from the rest of the company. When one is isolated this way, it is very difficult to be motivated and committed to the company goals.

Another one of these field trip meetings included the group with the very lowest language skills. During the preparation session they were very hesitant to construct questions they could ask the manager. However, when the meeting began, one of them asked about a situation at work that had been bothering her and a dam of unspoken questions was released. The manager responded warmly and nondefensively. It was quite an interactive session that facilitated an increase in positive perceptions of this manager. Until that time, the participant interaction with him had often been brief due to the level of noise on the manufacturing floor.

The success stories continue at both of the study sites. Pioneer has recently achieved ISO 9002 certification, receiving some of the highest scores that any company has received from Underwriters Laboratories (UL) auditors. The employees responded to auditor questions with confidence and skill. The manager of operations at Chino described the impact of BSTQ training on their ISO 9000 certification efforts:

> *Two years ago, if we had attempted the ISO certification process, we would have failed because the employees did not have the self-confidence. They were shy, hesitant, and afraid to ask questions. Since attending the training classes, the employees will talk to you; they're not afraid to ask questions. This year we can go to the floor and ask questions, and they feel confident to answer. They are openly involved in identifying improvements in work processes and they come up with ideas about safety and questions about what they can do. (These two areas were the focus of many hours of classroom work. It is very gratifying to know that the results are this visible to the manager.)*
>
> *Before the training, they would just take a whole box of parts when they needed some. After the training, they could read the instructions so they could identify the part by name and determine the correct quantity of parts to use. They understood why it was important to take only what they needed.*
>
> *There is more esprit de corps among the people now that they have been in classes together. The ping-*

pong table has become a meeting area; it is always full. Two years ago, no one played ping-pong together at break. They talk together now. The classes mixed the people together with others in the company and now they interact with each other more. They also can see the company's commitment to them as employees.

My major reason for writing this account of my experiences with BSTQ training is to share with you that you can improve employee understanding of TQM practices. This understanding will allow the employees to increase their skills in implementing these practices concurrently with basic workplace skills training. Deficiencies in basic workplace skills should not prohibit employees from being productive or participating in quality improvement or ISO 9000 certification efforts. These skills can be taught at a common sense level at the same time that basic skills are being taught. Providing these concepts in one integrated class helps to emphasize the practical application of both to the workplace.

Employees who have access to information and increasing knowledge and skills will contribute to the success of the organization willingly.

APPENDIX A

The Toro Company, Irrigation Division

BASIC SKILLS DISCOVERY

MATH SKILLS #1

Toro Irrigation Division
MATH ASSESSMENT

1. Count the items below. Write the total number on the line.

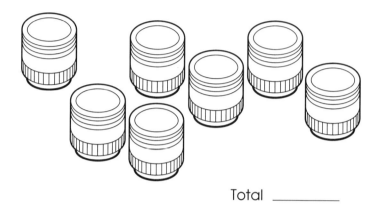

Total _____

2. Circle the part numbers that *do not* match this number: 665-06-65

665-06-65   665-06-65   665-06-65   665-06-65   665-06-65
665-06-65   665-60-65   665-06-65   665-06-65   656-06-65
665-06-65   665-06-65   665-06-56   665-06-65   665-06-65
665-06-65   665-06-65   665-06-65   665-06-65   665-06-65

3. Circle the invoice numbers that *do not* match their order number:

Invoice Number	*Order Number*
14F9117245	14F9117245
19E7664423	19E7684423
16G3559267	16G3559267
17H2584925	17H2584925
15J4700012	15J4790012

4. Count the marks and write the total number.

Reason for Reject	Number
Water leaking between cap, seal and riser	///
Cracked riser	ЖҬ //
Nozzle comes off	////
Would not rotate at any psi.	ЖҬ ЖҬ /
Total	

5. Find the total number of parts produced:

    1st Shift   234
    2nd Shift   365

        Total   _____

6. Add

45	18	436	965	2,636
+32	+93	+243	+226	+1,592

7. Subtract

16	75	567	638	3,527
−11	−26	−323	−529	−2,638

8. Multiply

32	62	52	75	246
×3	×5	×7	×34	×26

9. Divide

Circle the examples below that tell you to divide:

$12 \div 4 =$ $15 - 3 =$ $4/3 =$ $6\overline{)48}$ $7 \times 4 =$

Answer the following:

$7\overline{)21}$ $6\overline{)19}$ $4\overline{)26}$ $3\overline{)276}$ $5\overline{)365}$

10. Fractions

Change these fractions to whole or mixed numbers:

$12/3 =$ _____ $5/4 =$ _____ $6/2 =$ _____ $5/5 =$ _____

11. Circle the numbers that do not fall between 3.06 and 3.09.

3.05

3.075

3.16

3.07

3.082

3.26

12. Write how many hours and minutes have passed:

8:45 am to 11:15 am _____hrs. _____mins.

11:30 am to 2:55 pm _____hrs. _____mins.

13. Add the following numbers of minutes.

Minutes

26
14
22
<u>08</u>

Total Minutes _____

Change the minutes into hours.

Total _____Hours _____Minutes

14. Write the following as decimals:

66%   _____

23%   _____

37%   _____

15. Write the following as percents:

.05   _____   .15   _____

.25   _____   1   _____

16.

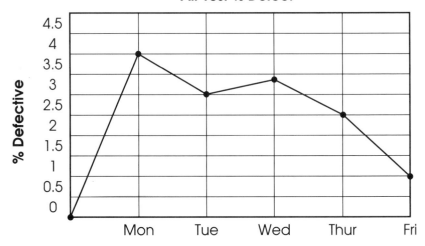

Air Test % Defect

a. On which day did we find the most defects? _____

b. On which day did we find the fewest defects? _____

c. What was the percentage of defects on Friday? _____

d. Circle the word that describes how the defects changed from Monday to Friday.

decreased

increased

e. Circle the day(s) when we had zero defects.

Monday

Tuesday

Wednesday

Thursday

Friday

None of the above

17. This is part of a control chart for a manufacturing process. Use the chart to answer the questions below it.

Key:
UCL = Upper Control Limit
X = Average
LCL = Lower Control Limit

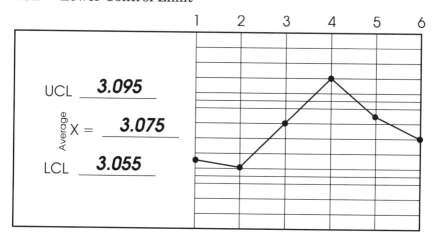

Use the control chart above to answer the following:

a. What is the upper control limit for this process? _____

b. What is the lower control limit for this process? _____

c. What is the average, or midpoint of the range? _____

d. On this chart, which dot tells us we might have a problem?

    Circle the number: 1   2   3   4   5

18. On the chart, record the measurements shown on the calipers below.

> Record measurement #1 in Sample Measurement 1
> Record measurement #2 in Sample Measurement 2
> Record measurement #3 in Sample Measurement 3
> Record measurement #4 in Sample Measurement 4

Find the sum, average, and range (subtract the lowest measurement from the highest.)

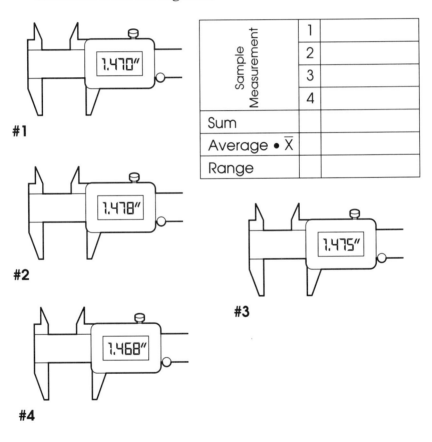

Sample Measurement		
	1	
	2	
	3	
	4	
Sum		
Average • X̄		
Range		

#1 — 1.470"

#2 — 1.478"

#3 — 1.475"

#4 — 1.468"

The Toro Company, Irrigation Division

BASIC SKILLS DISCOVERY
READING/WRITING #1

Name_____

Date_____

Toro Irrigation Division
READING/WRITING ASSESSMENT

1. Print the English alphabet.

_____

_____

_____

_____

_____

2. Finish these sentences:

a. I was born in _____.

b. I have lived in Riverside _____ years.

c. My job at Toro is to _____

_____.

d. One thing I would like to learn is _____

_____.

e. One thing I would like to do for fun is _____

_____

_____.

Vocabulary

What does each underlined word mean as it is used in the sentence? Put a check in the box by the words that tell you what it means.

3. Reject

   We *reject* products that have defects.

   ☐ shoot into space

   ☐ sell

   ☐ set aside

4. Insert

   We *insert* an adapter in pilot valves.

   ☐ place below

   ☐ place inside

   ☐ weld

5. Depress

   Depress fixture palm buttons until fixture releases.

   ☐ make sad

   ☐ look for

   ☐ push down

Vocabulary (Con't)

6. Manually

   Manually fit o-ring into nest of pilot valve body.
   ☐ quickly
   ☐ accurately
   ☐ with the hands

7. Slide

   Slide pilot valve housing over assembly.
   ☐ drop
   ☐ throw
   ☐ move sideways

8. Connect

   Connect the cables as you see in the picture.
   ☐ cross
   ☐ tie in knot
   ☐ to join one thing to another

Abbreviations

9. Find the abbreviation for each of the words below in the following list:

P/N, A/W, E/P FL., H.F.T., C/S, Nozz., USL, REV., FL., AVG., O/R, DIM., D/A, UCL, ACC., RET., P/C, W/C.

In the space after each of the following words, write the abbreviation.

Upper control limit _____

Deviation accepted _____

Average _____

Nozzle _____

Sequence

10. The following describes the process of turning in a labor card. The actions are out of order. Number them in the correct order (1 to 6) that you would perform them.

☐ Turn the card in to the supervisor at end of the week.

☐ At the end of each day, fill in the number of hours worked.

☐ Get new card.

☐ Sign the card.

☐ Supervisor signs the card.

☐ Supervisor sends the card to payroll.

11. Use the following information from a Toro memo to complete the statements below. There may be two correct answers. Check all of the right answers.

TO: Supervisors
FROM: Human Resources Department
SUBJECT: Vanpool

The first of our plans is the formation of a vanpool for long-distance commuters (from 30 to 40 miles). As a target group, we have selected the commuters from the Victorville/North San Bernardino areas to participate in this test project. Operation is expected to begin April 16.

The route will begin in Victorville, near the intersection of Highways 15 and 395. A stop will be made in San Bernardino at University Parkway/215 to pick up several other participating employees that reside in San Bernardino.

---

a. The vanpool will serve commuters from a distance of:

☐ 15–20 miles

☐ 20–30 miles

☐ 30–40 miles

b. The vanpool will make stops at:

☐ Victorville near Bear Valley Road and 395.

☐ Victorville at Highways 15 and 395 and University Parkway.

☐ Victorville near intersection of Highways 15 and 395.

☐ San Bernardino at intersection of Highway 215 and University Parkway.

12. Use the following adapted material to complete the statements below. There may be two correct answers. Check all of the right answers.

General Defect Specification for Plastic Parts

Contamination:

1. Black Specks: Specks that are noted in the part, molded into the plastic. If there are more specks than the customer requires, the part should be rejected. If no requirements have been given, any speck exceeding .050 inches in diameter within a .500 square inch, or any five specks that you can see within a half square inch, will be grounds for rejection.

---

   a. A part that has more specks than the customer requires should be:

      ☐ accepted.

      ☐ requested.

      ☐ rejected.

   b. If you don't know customer requirements, grounds for rejection are:

      ☐ five specks than can be seen within a half square inch.

      ☐ any speck larger than .050 inches in diameter within a .500 square inch.

      ☐ any speck you can see.

13. Use the following customer feedback form to answer the questions below:

Customer Feedback

TO:　　*Molding*

From (customer):　　Large Geared Heads

Part No./Name:　　*3-3501*

Product:　　*690 Body*

Problem:　　*Plugged bodies at the communication tube.*

　　Molded around July 2 or before.

Effect: *May cause rejects because units will not open if the*

tube is plugged.

---

a. When was the report written? _____

b. Who is the customer? _____

c. When was the defect noticed? _____

d. What could occur as a result of this problem? _____

_____

_____

PRINCIPLES OF WRITING BEHAVIORAL OBJECTIVES

Principle 1: Behavioral objectives are used only for describing the ends intended by the program, not the means.
  • Do not specify what the trainer will do.
  • Do not describe learner behavior during the task; focus on desired end behavior.
  • Describe objectives in behaviors that can be seen, heard, or touched.

Principle 2: The objectives for a program should reflect the different degrees of learning attainment it intends to produce.

Principle 3: Objectives may be written for participants as a group as well as for individuals.

Principle 4: In writing the objective, the verb should describe a specific action or behavior.

Writing Behavioral Objectives

A training objective describes the desired result to be achieved, when and by whom. An objective tells the following four things:

1. The performer (who).
2. The action or performance (what).
3. Time element (when).
4. Evaluation method (how will we know?).

When writing the objectives, use specific action words to describe the behavior.

Examples:

write	demonstrate	identify	compare
construct	list	build	replace
match	connect	select	compute

Write your own examples of action words that apply to the specific skills you are teaching:

_____	_____	_____
_____	_____	_____
_____	_____	_____
_____	_____	_____
_____	_____	_____
_____	_____	_____
_____	_____	_____

Writing Behavioral Objectives

Don't use vague verbs that are difficult to measure.

Examples:

know   understand   believe   appreciate

Be sure that the objectives are so specific that at the conclusion of the stated time period we can agree as to whether or not the objective has been accomplished.

Write three objectives for the course you are developing.

1. _____

_____

_____

2. _____

_____

_____

3. _____

_____

_____

Degrees of Learning

This classification describes, from simplest to most complex, six degrees to which information that is taught can be learned.

Degree of Learning	Definition
Knowledge	Recalling information pretty much as it was learned (rote learning).
Comprehension	Reporting information in a way other than how it was learned in order to show that it has been understood.
Application	Use of learned information to solve a problem.
Analysis	Taking learned information apart.
Synthesis	Creating something new and valuable, based on some criteria.
Evaluation	Judging the value of something for a particular purpose.

BSTQ Competencies

1.0 Job-related reading and writing competencies.

1.1 Read and interpret signs and safety posters.

1.3 Read and write simple safety instructions.

Safety Signs at Work

BSTQ 1
Competency 1.1, 1.3

Exercise 1

Objective for Exercise 1: After completing this exercise, the participants will be able to interpret the meaning of four safety signs with 100 percent accuracy.

Materials:

• Four workplace safety signs or posters.

• Worksheets for each participant with signs depicted.

Process:

• Discuss each sign with the group.

Suggested Questions:

• What does this sign mean?

• Where do you see it at work?

• What happens if you don't follow the safety rule?

• Has that ever happened?

• Why is it important to you to follow this safety rule?

Instruct learners to individually identify each sign on the worksheet, and write a sentence about why this safety rule needs to be followed.

Ask learners to read their sentences to the group or write them on the board.

Safety Signs at Work

In the spaces below, write what each sign means and why it is important.

1. _____
   _____
   _____

2. _____
   _____
   _____

3. _____
   _____
   _____

4. _____
   _____
   _____

BSTQ 1
Competency 1.1, 1.3

Exercise 2

Objective: In this exercise, participants will show that they comprehend the information in Exercise 1 by creating their own safety posters.

Materials:

• One flip chart page for each pair of learners.

• Colored markers that don't run through the page (enough for everyone to use a variety of colors.)

• Masking tape to mount posters on the wall.

Process:

* Direct participants to work in pairs to decide on a picture showing an important application of one of the safety rules. After mounting the posters on the wall, have each pair of participants explain their poster.

BSTQ 1
Competency 1.1, 1.3

Exercise 3

Objective: Participants will identify safety hazards in their area and suggest ways to make their jobs safer.

Materials:

* Notebook paper.

Process:

* Conduct a discussion on safety hazards in each individual work area. Focus discussion on actions learners can take to make their area safer. Have each learner write a description of the problem and their suggestion for solving the problem.

BSTQ 1
Competency 1.0, 1.2

Exercise 1

1.0 Job-related reading and writing.

1.2 Read, understand, use, and write work-related vocabulary (simple words, 2 or 3 word phrases.)

Objective: After completing this exercise, the participants will be able to identify, and describe in writing, short tasks at work.

Materials:

* Flip chart
* Markers
* Notebook paper

Process:

- The instructor will list on the flip chart, one at a time, action words elicited from the group that describe activities from the workplace. After each action word, ask for the name for the receiver of the action.

Example:

Action word   *Receiver of action*

assembles   speakers

calibrates   meters

Have the learners use a worksheet to fill in the words that complete this pattern. (Create a worksheet similar to the example below. Fill in random words using appropriate workplace vocabulary.)

Action Word	Receiver of Action

BSTQ 1
Competency 1.2

Exercise 2

Objective: Building on Exercise 1, participants will be able to describe the general steps in their job.

Materials:

- Flip chart
- Markers
- Worksheet
- Pencils

Process:

- Quickly review exercise 1.
- Give an example of the sequential steps in a common task.
- Ask participants to orally describe the actions they perform in their jobs.
- Have participants fill in the following worksheet.

Job Task Steps

In the blanks below, write a description of each step that you perform in your job in the order you perform it.

Step 1. _____

_____

Step 2. _____

_____

Step 3. _____

_____

Step 4. _____

_____

Step 5. _____

_____

Step 6. _____

_____

Job Task Steps Flowchart

Each of the steps in a process flowchart is shown by drawing a rectangle and labeling it. Your job is a process. Each of the steps can be shown as part of a flowchart.

In each of the boxes below, describe a step in your job (see Exercise 2). Write the steps in the order you do them.

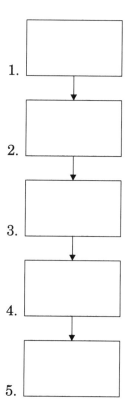

1.

2.

3.

4.

5.

INDEX